# VEGAN DESSERT COOKBOOK

# 100 VEGAN DESSERTS RECIPE BOOK

DIANA POLSKA

Copyright © 2017 by Diana Polska

All rights reserved. No part of this book may be reproduced or transmitted in any form or by any electronic or mechanical means, including photocopy, recording, or any information storage and retrieval system now known or to be invented, without written permission from the author, except by a reviewer who wishes to quote brief passages in connection with a review written for inclusion in a magazine, newspaper, website, or broadcast.

Disclaimer: Neither the author nor the publisher shall be held liable or responsible to any person or entity with respect to any loss or incidental or consequential damages caused, directly or indirectly, by the information or programs contained herein. You must seek the services of a competent professional before beginning any health or weight-loss advice. References are provided for informational purposes only. They do not constitute endorsements for websites or other sources.

# CONTENTS

**INTRO TO VEGANISM** ............................................................................................................6
   BECOMING VEGAN .........................................................................................................6
   BENEFITS OF A VEGAN DIET ..........................................................................................7
   GETTING ENOUGH PROTEIN ..........................................................................................8
   VEGAN FOOD IS DELICIOUS ...........................................................................................9

**RECIPES** ..............................................................................................................................10

### Chapter 1. Delicious Vegan Desserts for Spring ...............................................................11
   Vegan Spring Pie.............................................................................................................11
   Delicious Spring Chocolate Shake ..................................................................................12
   Vegan Lemon and Banana Bars .....................................................................................13
   Spring Vegan Sorbet .......................................................................................................14
   Spring Vegan Cheesecakes .............................................................................................15
   Poached Rhubarb ...........................................................................................................16
   Vegan Strawberry Cobbler ..............................................................................................17
   Chocolate and Avocado Pudding ....................................................................................18
   Vegan Spring Smoothie Bowl .........................................................................................19
   Spring Strawberry Crisp .................................................................................................20
   Vegan Chocolate Pie .......................................................................................................21
   Spring Vegan Ice Cream ..................................................................................................22
   Delicious Spring Fruit Cream .........................................................................................23
   Vegan Spring Donuts ......................................................................................................24
   Spring Vegan Poppy Seed Pancakes ..............................................................................25
   Special Spring Frozen Yogurt.........................................................................................26
   Spring Vegan Buckwheat Pancakes ...............................................................................27
   Vegan Cherry and Chocolate Parfait ..............................................................................28
   Vegan Lemon and Lavender Cake .................................................................................29
   Vegan Spring Brownies ..................................................................................................30
   Spring Peanut Butter Balls .............................................................................................32
   Vegan Spring Quinoa and Cocoa Bars ...........................................................................33
   Spring Apricot Crumble..................................................................................................34
   Springs Almond and Fig Granola Parfait ......................................................................35
   Vegan Chocolate Butter Cups ........................................................................................36

### Chapter 2. Delicious Vegan Desserts for Summer.............................................................37
   Summer Carrot Cake......................................................................................................37
   Salted Caramel Summer Ice Cream ..............................................................................38
   Vegan Sesame and Ginger Ice Cream ...........................................................................40
   Delicious Vegan Chia Seeds Pudding .............................................................................41
   Summer Mango and Coconut Sorbet ............................................................................42
   Vegan Chocolate Sorbet .................................................................................................43
   Amazing Vegan Summer Dessert ..................................................................................44

- Pineapple Upside Down Cake ............................................................................................... 45
- Vegan Summer Cake ............................................................................................................ 46
- Summer Lemon Fudge ......................................................................................................... 48
- Summer Raw Fudge ............................................................................................................. 49
- Summer Tahini Dessert ........................................................................................................ 50
- Delicious Vegan Raspberry Truffles ..................................................................................... 51
- Vegan Summer Pops ............................................................................................................ 52
- Tasty Summer Avocado Truffles .......................................................................................... 53
- Summer Vegan Bars ............................................................................................................. 54
- Vegan Chocolate Cookie Dough Bites .................................................................................. 55
- Simple Vegan Summer Tart .................................................................................................. 56
- Vegan Frozen Banana Popsicles ........................................................................................... 57
- Vegan Twinkies with Tasty Coconut Filling ......................................................................... 58
- Tasty Vegan Root Beer Cupcakes ......................................................................................... 59
- Vegan Almond Bundt Cake .................................................................................................. 60

## Chapter 3. Delicious Autumn Vegan Desserts ............................................................63
- Pumpkin and Quinoa Cookies ............................................................................................... 63
- Delicious Vegan Apple Cake ................................................................................................ 64
- Apple and Maple Crisp ......................................................................................................... 66
- Amazing Vegan Gingerbread Cake ....................................................................................... 67
- Vegan Pumpkin Bread .......................................................................................................... 68
- Vegan Apricot Muffins ......................................................................................................... 69
- Apple and Nuts Tart .............................................................................................................. 70
- Apple and Cider Bread .......................................................................................................... 71
- Autumn Pumpkin and Pecan Granola ................................................................................... 72
- Vegan Pecan Scones ............................................................................................................. 73
- Vegan Pumpkin Spice Donuts ............................................................................................... 74
- Vegan Chocolate and Chickpea Blondies ............................................................................. 75
- Special Strawberry and Rhubarb Pie .................................................................................... 76
- Vegan Apple Cheesecake ...................................................................................................... 77
- Vegan Black Bean Brownies ................................................................................................ 79
- Autumn Vegan Coconut Macaroons ..................................................................................... 80
- Vegan Blueberry and Rosemary Dessert .............................................................................. 81
- Vegan Raspberry and Corn Muffins ..................................................................................... 82
- Vegan Ganache Cake ............................................................................................................ 83
- Vegan Saffron Pudding ......................................................................................................... 84
- Vegan Sweet Potato Pudding ................................................................................................ 85
- Autumn Vegan Chocolate Pudding ....................................................................................... 86
- A True Vegan Pumpkin Pudding .......................................................................................... 87
- Autumn Vegan Bread Pudding ............................................................................................. 88
- Vegan Pumpkin Smoothie ..................................................................................................... 89

## Chapter 4. Vegan Desserts for Winter .........................................................................90
- Vegan Ice Cream Sandwich .................................................................................................. 90

- Delicious Vegan Pomegranate Fudge .................................................................................. 92
- Vegan Caramel Apples ........................................................................................................ 93
- Vegan Winter Cheesecake .................................................................................................. 94
- Winter Pumpkin Custard ..................................................................................................... 95
- Vegan Chestnut and Cashew Trifles .................................................................................... 96
- Winter Berry and Cashew Cake ........................................................................................... 98
- Winter Vegan Fruit Jelly ....................................................................................................... 99
- Vegan Winter Couscous Delight ........................................................................................ 100
- Vegan Almond and Fig Winter Dessert ............................................................................. 101
- Vegan Winter Sponge Cake ............................................................................................... 102
- Special Winter Cherry Sorbet ............................................................................................ 104
- Winter Persimmon Bars .................................................................................................... 105
- Winter Vegan Crème Brule ............................................................................................... 107
- Vegan Tomato and Chocolate Cupcakes .......................................................................... 108
- Winter Vegan Tomato Cake .............................................................................................. 109
- Winter Nectarines and Olive Oil Cake .............................................................................. 110
- Vegan Butternut Cake ....................................................................................................... 111
- Winter Vegan Rum Cake ................................................................................................... 113
- Winter Vanilla Cake ........................................................................................................... 114
- Winter Marmalade Cake ................................................................................................... 115
- Winter Green Apple Pie Smoothie .................................................................................... 116
- Winter Coconut and Clementine Smoothie ..................................................................... 117

# INTRO TO VEGANISM

A vegan diet consists of only plant-derived foods. Vegans don't consume any animal-derived food including meat (land or sea animals), milk, eggs, or honey. They also don't wear or use any animal-derived products such as leather, snakeskin, fur, silk, wool, cosmetics and soaps.

A vegan diet is extremely beneficial for the environment and for animals. Going vegan can also improve health dramatically for some people. A vegan diet has even been shown to reverse some illnesses such as heart disease and cancer.

Many people choose to become vegan as a way of accepting responsibility for their own personal health as well as for the well-being of animals and the environment and to promote a more humane and caring world. Many vegans believe they have an obligation to try to do their best in this world even if others don't have the same point of view.

## BECOMING VEGAN

There are several "levels" of vegetarianism. Starting from the most restrictive and working our way down, the types of vegetarian are as follows:

- Vegan: Vegans do not consume any animal products or by-products such as meat, fish, poultry, eggs and dairy. Vegans do not use honey or beeswax, gelatin, and any other animal by-product ingredients or products. Vegans typically do not use animal products such as leather, fur, silk, and wool.

- Lacto-vegetarian: Lacto-vegetarians do not eat meat, fish, poultry or eggs. However, lactovegetarians do consume dairy products such as cheese, milk, and yogurt.

- Ovo-vegetarian: Ovo-vegetarians do not eat meat, fish, poultry or dairy products. However, ovo-vegetarians do consume eggs.

- Lacto-ovo vegetarian: Lacto-ovo vegetarians do not consume meat, fish or poultry. However, lacto-ovo vegetarians do consume dairy products and egg products. This is the most common type of vegetarianism.

- Pollotarian: This semi-vegetarian diet restricts meat consumption to chicken or other poultry. The "pollo" prefix in pollotarian literally refers to the word "chicken."

Pollotarians do not consume red meat. They may or may not also exclude fish, seafood, eggs and dairy from their diet.

- Pescatarian (also spelled pescetarian): Pescatarians restrict their meat consumption to fish and seafood only. Pescatarians do not consume meat or poultry. Some pescatarians (known as lacto-ovo-pescatarian) consume eggs and dairy products while others do not.

- Flexitarian: A plant-based diet with occasional meat consumption. A flexitarian does their best to limit meat intake as much as possible and they have an almost entirely plant-based diet.

When starting out, most people slowly work their way toward becoming vegan. They start out as flexitarian or pescatarian and slowly work their way toward becoming completely vegan.

Organizations such as PETA (www.peta.org) have exposed the extreme brutality and cruelty toward animals used for food and animal-derived products. Many people become educated through organizations such as PETA, and documentaries, on the benefits of veganism before making an informed decision to become vegan.

## BENEFITS OF A VEGAN DIET

Several documentaries investigate in-depth and provide compelling evidence on the benefits of a vegan diet regarding personal health, prevention of animal cruelty, and saving the environment.

*Forks over Knives* (2011) discusses how easy it is to prevent and even reverse many diseases with a plant-based diet, rather than drugs and surgery.

*Vegucated* (2011) is a socio-comical documentary about 3 omnivore New York guys who plan to go vegan for six weeks for weight loss and other health benefits. During their vegan journey, they uncover the dark side of animal agriculture.

*Farm to Fridge* (2011), at only 12 minutes long, reveals undercover footage of cruelty toward animals used for food from some of the nation's largest factory farms.

*Cowspiracy* (2014) reveals that meat production is the number one destroyer of the environment through the use of unsustainable farming practices. A few facts in the film are startling and eye-opening (www.cowspiracy.com/facts/). Animal agriculture is responsible for 18 percent of greenhouse gas emissions, more than the combined exhaust from all transportation. Livestock and their by-products account for at least 32,000 million tons of carbon dioxide (CO2) per year or 51% of all worldwide greenhouse gas emissions.

## GETTING ENOUGH PROTEIN

Those that are firm believers that humans do not need any animal protein should not push a vegan diet on anyone. A vegan diet is a personal choice that works for some but doesn't work for everyone.

Not everyone is designed exactly the same and just like every single individual has a different fingerprint, everyone needs a diet tailored to the individual needs of their body. Some people do well on a vegan diet for their entire lifetime while others may need some animal protein in their diet. Animal protein is a source of concentrated protein, fat-soluble vitamins and fat-soluble activators that are not are readily available from plant foods. Animals considered strictly vegetarian and vegan like rabbits, elephants, hippos, rhinos, bison, horses and deer actually consume insects that adhere to the plants that they eat.

The amount of concentrated protein needed by each person varies. Some people require a lot of protein, while others do not produce enough hydrochloric acid in their stomachs to handle meat intake well.

Those on a vegan diet can get enough protein if they include vegan sources of protein in their diet. Vegans can get enough protein from lentils, tempeh, beans, nuts, and seeds. Consuming edible insects such as crickets is an alternative way to get more than enough protein. Many insects are rich in protein and good fats and high in calcium, iron, and zinc.

In the future, to sustain the expected growth of population, we will be forced to eat less meat, dairy, and eggs and seek alternative sources of protein. It is widely accepted that by 2050, the world will host 9 billion people. To accommodate this number, current food production will need to double. Land is scarce and expanding the area devoted to farming is rarely a viable or sustainable option.

There are huge environmental benefits of consuming edible insects for food. Crickets, for example, require only 2 kilograms of feed for every 1 kilogram of bodyweight gain. Insects are reported to emit fewer greenhouse gasses and less ammonia than cows or pigs, and they require significantly less land and water than cattle rearing.

Protein powders are not a recommended source of protein. Isolated protein powder or vegetable protein is inferior in quality. Protein powder made from soy, whey, casein or eggs is made by a high-temperature process that denatures the protein, causing it to have nitrates and other carcinogens. Soy protein is high in phytates that block mineral absorption, phytoestrogens that depress the thyroid, and enzyme inhibitors that cause cancer. (Rackis, J. J. (1985). Qualitative Plant Foods in Human Nutrition, 35, 225)

Those on a vegan diet need to ensure they are getting enough iron, Vitamin B-12, Omega-3 and Vitamin D. Everyone, including vegans, should take a "vitamin/mineral whole food supplement" to prevent any nutritional deficiencies. Whole food supplements are made from concentrated whole foods. Isolated nutrients or synthetic nutrients are not natural, meaning they are never found by themselves in nature. A whole food supplement is readily absorbed by the body, while synthetic vitamin/mineral supplements are not.

## VEGAN FOOD IS DELICIOUS

Those that think going vegan consists of eating only fruits, vegetables and soybeans will be surprised at just how appealing vegan food can be. Many restaurants and food manufacturers are making vegan dessert ingredient alternatives taste even more delicious than regular desserts.

There are thousands of testimonials of people who actually prefer the taste of vegan desserts. There are so many vegan desserts: Vegan cookies, non-dairy ice-cream, cakes, cupcakes, pies; the list goes on.

# RECIPES

# Chapter 1. Delicious Vegan Desserts for Spring

## Vegan Spring Pie
There's nothing better than a tasty vegan pie in the spring!

Ingredients:
2 tablespoons of spelt flour
2 tablespoons of soft vegan buttery spread
2 tablespoons of lime juice
A pinch of lime zest
½ cup of organic sugar
1 ½ tablespoons of arrowroot powder
3 cups of fresh blackberries
2 cups of strawberries
1 vegan pie crust, made with spelt flour

Directions:
1. In a bowl, mix vegan buttery spread with flour, organic sugar, arrowroot powder, lime juice, lime zest, blackberries, and strawberries.
2. Roll your pie crust dough and divide it into 2 balls.
3. Arrange the first ball evenly in a pie pan, pour the mix you've just made, and top with evenly layered thin strips from the second ball of dough.
4. Put your pie in the oven at 400 degrees F and bake for 30 minutes.
5. Reduce heat to 350 degrees F and bake for 30 minutes more.
6. Take pie out of the oven and leave it aside to completely cool down before serving it.
Enjoy!

Nutritional value: 250 calories, 0 grams of fat, 0 grams of carbs, 0 grams of fiber, 3 grams of sugar

# Delicious Spring Chocolate Shake
It's healthy and it's 100% vegan! What more do you want?

Ingredients:
2 medium size bananas
2 teaspoons of raw cocoa powder
½ big avocado, mashed
¾ cup of soy milk
A pinch of salt

Directions:
1. Put bananas in your kitchen blender and pulse a few times.
2. Add cocoa powder, avocado and a pinch of salt. Pulse again.
4. Add soy milk, pulse a few more seconds, transfer the mix to a glass and serve right away.
Enjoy!

Nutritional value: 285 calories, 13 grams of fat, 37 grams of carbs, 1 gram of fiber, 8 grams of protein

## Vegan Lemon and Banana Bars
It's one of the most amazing combinations ever!

Ingredients:
1 cup of coconut oil
1 ½ bananas, chopped
A pinch of salt
1/3 cup of agave syrup
¼ cup of lemon juice
A pinch of lemon zest
3 kiwis, chopped
Raw hemp seeds for the crust

Directions:
1. In your food processor, mix bananas with kiwis, coconut oil, a pinch of salt, agave syrup, lemon juice, and a pinch of lemon zest. Pulse well.
2. Grease a pan with some coconut oil, spread hemp seeds on the bottom, pour mix over, put food in the fridge for 30 minutes, slice, and serve bars.
Enjoy!

Nutritional value: 163 calories, 37 grams of fat, 15 grams of carbs, 10 grams of sugar, 1 gram of fiber

# Spring Vegan Sorbet
It's a vegan dessert you should really try this spring!

Ingredients:
1 cup of dates, pitted and chopped
3 cups of plums, chopped
A pinch of salt
2 ½ cups of water
1 teaspoon of lemon juice

Directions:
1. Put dates and plums in your food processor, add a pinch of salt and blend well.
2. Gradually add water and pulse a few more times.
3. Add lemon juice, pulse for a few more seconds, transfer the mix to a bowl and keep the sorbet in the freezer for 2 hours.
4. Scoop into dessert cups and serve right away!
Enjoy!

Nutritional value: 85 calories, 0 grams of fat, 23 grams of carbs, 0 grams of fiber, 1 gram of sugar, 1 gram of protein

# Spring Vegan Cheesecakes
Think about how happy you'll make everyone with this vegan dessert!

Ingredients:
*For the crust:*
½ cup of pecans
½ cup of macadamia nuts
½ cup of dates
½ cup of walnuts
A pinch of salt
*For the filling:*
1 cup of date paste
3 cups of cashews, soaked for 3 hours
½ cup of almond milk
2 cups of strawberries
¾ cup of coconut oil
¼ cup of lime juice
*For serving:*
Sliced limes for serving
Sliced strawberries for serving

Directions:
1. Put nuts, walnuts, dates, pecans and a pinch of salt in your food processor, and blend well.
2. Put 3 spoons of crust mix into each muffin tin, press well, and leave aside for now.
3. Put cashews, strawberries, date paste, lime juice, almond milk and coconut oil in your food processor, and blend well.
4. Put 3 spoons of filling mix on top of the crust mix, then put the mix in the freezer and keep for 2 hours.
5. Transfer cheesecakes onto a platter, top with strawberries and limes, and serve.
Enjoy!

Nutritional value: 140 calories, 2 grams of fat, 22 grams of carbs, 0 grams of fiber, 12 grams of sugar, 2 grams of protein

## Poached Rhubarb
It is so delicious! We love it and you will enjoy it for sure!

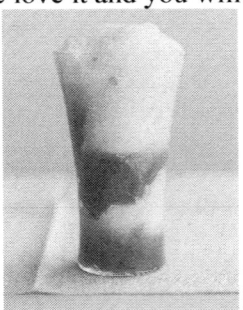

Ingredients:
Juice from 1 lemon
Some thin lemon zest strips
1 ½ cup of palm sugar
A pinch of salt
4 ½ cups of rhubarbs, cut into medium pieces.
1 vanilla bean
1 ½ cups of water
Vegan ice cream for serving

Directions:
1. Put the water in a pan.
2. Add palm sugar, vanilla bean, lemon juice, a pinch of salt and lemon zest.
3. Stir, bring to a boil and add rhubarb.
4. Reduce heat, simmer for 5 minutes, take off heat and transfer rhubarb into a bowl.
5. Allow liquid to cool down, discard vanilla bean and serve it with your favorite vegan ice cream. Enjoy!

Nutritional value: 108 calories, 1 gram of fat, 0 grams of carbs, 0 grams of fiber, 1 gram of sugar, 0 grams of protein

# Vegan Strawberry Cobbler
It's a delicate and elegant spring dessert that you'll really like!

Ingredients:
¾ cup of palm sugar
6 cups of strawberries, cut into halves
1/8 teaspoon of baking powder
1 tablespoon of lemon juice
½ cup of spelt flour
1/8 teaspoon of baking soda
A pinch of salt
½ cup of water
3 ½ tablespoons vegetable shortening
Vegetable cooking spray

Directions:
1. Spray a baking dish with some oil and leave aside.
2. In a bowl, mix strawberries with half of palm sugar. Sprinkle some flour and add lemon juice.
3. Stir well and pour the mix into a baking dish.
4. In another bowl, mix flour with the rest of the palm sugar, a pinch of salt, baking powder and soda. Stir well.
5. Add shortening and mix until the whole thing crumbles in your hands.
6. Add ½ cup of water over strawberries.
7. Put food in the oven at 375 degrees F and bake for 30 minutes.
8. Take cobbler out of the oven, leave aside for 10 minutes and then serve.

Enjoy!

Nutritional value: 275 calories, 9 grams of fat, 48 grams of carbs, 3 grams of protein, 4 grams of fiber, 33 grams of sugar

## Chocolate and Avocado Pudding
You won't stop eating it!

Ingredients:
1 cup of almond milk
2 avocados, peeled
¾ cup of cocoa powder
1 teaspoon of vanilla extract
¾ cup of maple syrup
¼ teaspoon of cinnamon
A pinch of salt
Walnuts chopped for serving

Directions:
1. Put avocados in your kitchen blender, and pulse well.
2. Add cocoa powder, almond milk, maple syrup, cinnamon, a pinch of salt and vanilla extract, and pulse well again.
3. Pour the mix into serving bowls. Top with walnuts and keep in the fridge for 2-3 hours before you serve it.

Enjoy!

Nutritional value: 231 calories, 14 grams of fat, 27 grams of carbs, 20, grams of sugar, 6 grams of fiber, 2 grams of protein

# Vegan Spring Smoothie Bowl
It's easy and totally delicious!

Ingredients:
½ cup of coconut water
1 ½ cup of avocado, chopped
1 big banana
2 tablespoons of green tea powder
2 teaspoons of lime zest
1 tablespoon of palm sugar
Melted coconut butter for serving
1 mango thinly sliced for serving

Directions:
1. In your blender, mix water with banana, avocado, green tea powder, and lime zest. Pulse well.
2. Add palm sugar, and pulse well again.
3. Transfer the mix into a bowl, top with coconut butter, add sliced mango, and serve.
Enjoy!

Nutritional value: 437 calories, 22 grams of fat, 55 grams of carbs, 31 grams of sugar, 10 grams of fiber, 10 grams of protein

# Spring Strawberry Crisp

You are about to learn how to make one of the best vegan spring desserts ever!

Ingredients:
*For the filling:*
3 teaspoons of cornstarch
1 ¼ cup of strawberries, chopped
3 tablespoons of maple syrup
1 ¼ cups of blueberries, chopped
¼ teaspoon of cinnamon
A pinch of salt
A pinch of ginger, grated
½ teaspoon of vanilla
*For the topping:*
A drizzle of vegetable oil for greasing the pan
3 tablespoons of raw cane sugar
3 tablespoons of almond flour
¾ cup of rolled oats
1/3 cup of almonds, chopped
A pinch of salt
3 tablespoons of vegan butter
¼ teaspoon of cinnamon

Directions:
1. In a bowl, mix strawberries with blueberries, maple syrup, cornstarch, ¼ teaspoon of cinnamon, vanilla, a pinch of salt and a pinch of grated ginger. Mix well.
2. In another bowl, mix rolled oats with almond flour, raw cane sugar, almonds, a pinch of salt, ¼ teaspoon of cinnamon and the vegan butter. Mix well with your hands.
3. Pour berry mix into a greased pan, sprinkle topping mix on top, put the food in the oven at 475 degrees F and bake for 30 minutes.
4. Take dessert out of the oven, then leave aside to completely cool down before serving it. Enjoy!

Nutritional value: 318 calories, 12 grams of fat, 6 grams of fiber, 53 grams of carbs, 3 grams of sugar, 6 grams of protein

# Vegan Chocolate Pie

Ingredients:
12 ounces of extra firm tofu
3 tablespoons of rice milk
1 ½ teaspoons of vanilla extract
A pinch of salt
1 ½ cups of vegan chocolate chips
2 tablespoons of maple syrup
1 vegan graham cracker crust
*For the vegan graham cracker crust:*
¼ cup of coconut oil, already melted
12 graham crackers
2 tablespoons of organic brown sugar

Directions:
1. Put crackers and brown sugar in your blender, and pulse well.
2. Add coconut oil, and pulse for another few seconds.
3. Transfer mix to a pie crust pan. Spread, press well, then it put the food in the oven at 375 degrees F and bake for 10 minutes.
4. Take pie crust out of the oven and leave it aside to cool down.
5. Meanwhile, in a bowl, mix vanilla with tofu, salt, rice milk and maple syrup. Stir well.
6. Transfer the mix to your food processor, and pulse well.
7. Melt vegan chocolate chips in your broiler, add to tofu mix, and stir well.
8. Pour this into the pie crust, then put the food in the freezer, wait 2 hours, and then serve it.
Enjoy!

Nutritional value: 353 calories, 18 grams of fat, 46 grams of carbs, 2 grams of fiber, 12 grams of sugar, 5 grams of protein

# Spring Vegan Ice Cream
It may sound more like a summertime dessert idea, it's perfect in the spring!

Ingredients:
1 tablespoon of arrowroot starch
2 cans of coconut milk
¼ teaspoon of vanilla beans
1 tablespoon of vodka
1/3 cup of pure cane sugar
1/3 cup of coconut nectar

Directions:
1. Fill 1/3 of a bowl with ice cubes, place another bowl on top and leave aside for now.
2. Pour coconut milk in a pot, reserve 2 tablespoons, put them in a bowl, mix with arrowroot starch, and stir well.
3. Add arrowroot mix to coconut milk in the pot, and stir.
4. Add vanilla beans, cane sugar and coconut nectar. Stir well, then place the pot on the stove and heat it up over medium heat.
5. Stir well, bring to a boil, boil for 2 minutes, take off heat, and then pour the mix into the bowl that you've placed over the ice.
6. Add vodka, stir well and leave aside for 1 hour and 30 minutes.
7. Pour this into your ice cream machine and turn on.
8. Pour the mix into a container, then put it in the freezer and leave it there for 20 minutes.
9. Serve right away!
Enjoy!

Nutritional value: 136 calories, 4 grams of fat, 20 grams of carbs, 1 gram of fiber, 18 grams of sugar, 1 gram of protein

# Delicious Spring Fruit Cream
It's the best combination of ingredients! Try it!

Ingredients:
1 cup of apples, chopped
1 cup of pineapple, chopped
1 cup of banana, chopped
1 cup of sapodilla fruit, chopped
1 cup of melon, chopped
1 cup of papaya, chopped
½ teaspoon of vanilla powder
¾ cup of cashews
Stevia to taste
Some cold water

Directions:
1. Put cashews in a bowl, add some water on top, leave aside for 6 hours, drain them and put them in your food processor.
2. Blend them well and add cold water to cover them.
3. Also, add stevia and vanilla, blend some more and keep in the fridge for now.
4. In a bowl, arrange a layer of mixed apples with bananas, pineapples, melon, papaya and sapodilla fruit.
5. Add a layer of cold cashew paste, another layer of fruits, another layer of cashew paste, and top with a layer of fruits.
6. Serve right away!

Enjoy!

Nutritional value: 140 calories, 1 gram of fat, 3 grams of carbs, 0 grams of fiber, 1 gram of sugar, 2 grams of protein

# Vegan Spring Donuts
The perfect spring dessert is here! Try these amazing donuts today!

Ingredients:
1/3 cup of vegetable oil
2 cups of soy milk
½ cup of palm sugar
1/3 cup of maple syrup
A pinch of salt
1 package of dry yeast
5 cups of organic flour
4 tablespoons of vegan butter
½ cup of brown sugar

Directions:
1. Put soy milk in a pot.
2. Add oil, maple syrup and palm sugar. Stir and bring to a boil.
3. Take off heat and leave aside for 30 minutes.
4. In a bowl, mix 4 ¾ cups of flour with a pinch of salt and yeast. Stir well.
5. Add this mixture to the milk mixture. Stir well again and leave the combination aside in a warm place for 1 hour.
6. Knead your dough and leave it aside for 10 or more minutes.
7. Transfer dough to a working surface, shape 2 inch balls, arrange them in a greased baking dish and leave them aside for a few minutes.
8. Put them in the oven at 350 degrees F and bake them for 10 minutes.
9. Take donuts out of the oven and leave them aside for a few minutes to cool down.
10. In a bowl, mix vegan butter with a ¼ cup of flour and brown sugar. Stir well and pour evenly over donuts.

Enjoy!

Nutritional value: 115 calories, 4 grams of fat, 18 grams of carbs, 8 grams of sugar, 0 grams of fiber, 1 gram of protein

# Spring Vegan Poppy Seed Pancakes
These will be the best pancakes ever!

Ingredients:
1 tablespoon of lemon juice
Zest from 2 lemons
2 cups of almond milk
1 teaspoon of almond extract
1 teaspoon of vanilla extract
1 cup of whole wheat flour
1/3 cup of oat bran
2/3 cups of all-purpose flour
1 ½ teaspoon of baking powder
2 tablespoons of sugar
A pinch of salt
¼ cup of vegetable oil
½ cup of silver almonds

Directions:
1. In a bowl, mix almond milk with lemon zest, lemon juice, vanilla extract, poppy seeds and almond extract. Stir very well.
2. In another bowl, mix all-purpose flour with whole wheat flour, a pinch of salt, oat bran, and baking powder. Stir well.
3. Add vegetable oil to the first mix, and stir well again.
4. Pour this mix over the flour mix and stir until they combine.
5. Add almonds and stir again.
6. Heat up a pan over medium-high heat, grease with some vegetable oil, drop 1/3 cup of pancakes batter, spread evenly, cook for 2 minutes, flip and cook another 2 minutes, transfer to a plate, and leave aside.
7. Repeat the previous step with the rest of the batter, and serve pancakes right away.

Enjoy!

Nutritional value: 80 calories, 1 gram of fat, 15 grams of carbs, 2 grams of fiber, 1 gram of sugar, 3 grams of protein

# Special Spring Frozen Yogurt
## It's really simple to make, and it tastes great!

Ingredients:
½ cup of frozen raspberries
2 tablespoons of water
¼ cup of maple syrup
2 cups of coconut yogurt, homemade
¼ cup of shredded and unsweetened coconut
½ teaspoon of vanilla extract

Directions:
1. Put raspberries in a pot, add water, heat the pot over medium heat, mash berries, and cook for 2 minutes.
2. Strain into a bowl, discard seeds, and mix with maple syrup, coconut yogurt, vanilla extract and shredded coconut. Stir well.
3. Transfer this into your ice cream maker and turn the machine on.
4. When it's done, transfer the frozen yogurt to a container and keep the yogurt in the freezer until it's ready to be served.

Enjoy!

Nutritional value: 150 calories, 6 grams of fat, 0 grams of carbs, 6 grams of fiber, 0 grams of sugar, 10 grams of protein

# Spring Vegan Buckwheat Pancakes
It's a delightful dessert idea for you and your loved ones!

Ingredients:
½ cup of buckwheat flour
1 cup of almond milk
1 tablespoon of vegetable oil
1 tablespoon of ground flax seeds
1 teaspoon of vanilla extract
½ cup of spelt flour
A pinch of salt
1 teaspoon of baking powder
½ teaspoon of cinnamon
Maple syrup for serving

Directions:
1. In a bowl, mix oil with milk, vanilla, and flaxseeds. Stir and leave aside for 5 minutes.
2. In another bowl, mix buckwheat flour with spelt flour, cinnamon, a pinch of salt and baking powder. Stir again.
3. Mix wet ingredients with dry ones, and stir well.
4. Grease a pan with some oil, heat the pan over medium heat, pour ¼ cup of pancakes batter, spread, cook for 3 minutes, flip and cook 2 more minutes, and transfer to a plate.
5. Repeat this with the rest of the batter. Arrange all pancakes on a platter and serve them with some maple syrup on top.

Enjoy!

Nutritional value: 240 calories, 13 grams of fat, 41 grams of carbs, 8 grams of fiber, 0 grams of sugar, 12 grams of protein

# Vegan Cherry and Chocolate Parfait
You won't believe the taste this parfait has!

Ingredients:
½ cup of old-fashioned oats
2 tablespoons of cocoa powder
1 cup of almond milk
1 tablespoon of chia seeds
A pinch of salt
½ teaspoon of vanilla extract

Directions:
1. In a bowl, mix oats with cocoa powder, almond milk, a pinch of salt, vanilla extract and chia seeds. Stir well until the ingredients blend.
2. Transfer the mix into a dessert glass, then put it in the fridge, wait 2 hours, and then serve. Enjoy!

Nutritional value: 130 calories, 10 grams of fat, 23 grams of carbs, 2 grams of fiber, 3 grams of sugar, 15 grams of protein

# Vegan Lemon and Lavender Cake
## The taste is simply wonderful!

Ingredients:
1 teaspoon of baking powder
1 ½ cup of spelt flour
½ teaspoon of cassava flour
½ cup of vegan coconut yogurt
2 tablespoons of ground flax seeds, mixed with 6 tablespoons of water
Juice from 1 lemon
Zest from 1 lemon
½ cup of soft vegan butter
1 teaspoon of vanilla extract
1 tablespoon of culinary lavender
1/3 cup of maple syrup

Directions:
1. In a bowl, mix flour with cassava and baking powder. Stir well.
2. In a bowl, mix butter with maple syrup, and stir using your kitchen mixer.
3. Add flax seeds mixed with water, vanilla, and half of the flour mix. Stir again well.
4. Add half of the coconut yogurt and stir some more.
5. Add the rest of the flour, the rest of the yogurt, lemon juice, and zest. Mix well.
6. Add lavender, stir gently, pour the batter into a loaf pan lined with parchment paper, put the food in the oven at 350 degrees and bake for 40 minutes.
7. Take cake out of the oven, leave aside for 10 minutes to cool down, transfer to a platter, slice and serve.

Enjoy!

Nutritional value: 280 calories, 10 grams of fat, 45 grams of carbs, 1 gram of fiber, 25 grams of sugar, 2 grams of protein

# Vegan Spring Brownies
## Enjoy this season with some tasty brownies!

Ingredients:
*For the brownies:*
½ cup of oat flour
¼ teaspoon of baking powder
¼ cup of coconut flour
2 tablespoons of cocoa powder
1 tablespoon of flax meal
¼ cup of maple syrup
2 tablespoons of almond milk
1/3 cup of vegan chocolate
1 teaspoon of vanilla extract
2 tablespoons of coconut oil
1 teaspoon of ground coffee, soaked
2 tablespoons of raw sugar
2 tablespoons vegan chocolate chips
*For the cheesecake:*
2 tablespoons coconut flour
8 ounces of firm tofu
1 teaspoon of vanilla extract
2 tablespoons of coconut oil
3 tablespoons of raw sugar
2 tablespoons of lemon juice

Directions:
1. In a bowl, mix ½ cup of oat flour with 2 tablespoons of cocoa powder, ¼ teaspoon of baking powder, ¼ cup of coconut flour, and stir well.
2. Put 2 tablespoons of almond milk in a pot. Heat up over medium-high heat.
3. Add flax meal, ¼ cup of maple syrup, 1/3 cup of vegan chocolate, 1 teaspoon of vanilla extract, 1 teaspoon of coffee, 2 tablespoons of coconut oil, 2 tablespoons of raw sugar and vegan chocolate chips. Stir and cook for a few minutes.
4. Pour this over the dry ingredients, stir well and then pour batter into a pan lined with parchment paper.
5. Meanwhile, press tofu well, then place it in your food processor and blend it well.

6. Add 2 tablespoons of coconut flour, 2 tablespoons of coconut oil, 3 tablespoons of raw sugar, 1 teaspoon of vanilla extract and 2 tablespoons of lemon juice. Pulse again well.
7. Pour this over the batter in the pan, spread evenly in a thin layer, then put the food in the oven at 350 degrees F and bake for 45 minutes.
8. Take cake out of the oven, leave aside to cool down, slice, arrange on a platter and serve. Enjoy!

Nutritional value: 300 calories, 16 grams of fat, 34 grams of carbs, 2 grams of fiber, 24 grams of sugar, 3 grams of protein

## Spring Peanut Butter Balls
They even taste better than they look!

Ingredients:
½ cup of walnuts, finely ground
½ cup of oat flour
¼ cup of raw cocoa powder
1 teaspoon of vanilla extract
3 tablespoons of flaxseeds, finely ground
2 tablespoons of peanut butter
¼ cup of maple syrup
3 teaspoons of water
¼ cup of coconut, shredded

Directions:
1. In your kitchen blender, mix oat flour with walnuts, flax seeds, and cocoa powder. Pulse well.
2. Add maple syrup and vanilla, and pulse a few more times.
3. Add water and peanut butter, pulse again, transfer the mix into a bowl and shape 10 balls.
4. Put shredded coconut in a bowl, roll each ball in it, arrange on a plate and serve them right away.

Enjoy!

Nutritional value: 80 calories, 4, 6 grams of carbs, 1 gram of fiber, 1 gram of sugar, 3 grams of protein

# Vegan Spring Quinoa and Cocoa Bars
They taste divine!

Ingredients:
¼ cup of extra virgin coconut oil
2 tablespoons of cocoa and mint syrup
¾ cup of cocoa butter
¼ teaspoon of vanilla extract
1 cup of cocoa powder
¼ teaspoon of peppermint extract
¼ cup of quinoa, already cooked and puffed
¼ cup of cocoa nibs

Directions:
1. Heat up a pan with the cocoa butter over medium-high heat. Melt it and mix it with cocoa and mint syrup and coconut oil.
2. Stir well, cook until it melts, then take it off the heat and mix it with peppermint and vanilla.
3. Pour this into a bowl, add cocoa powder, and stir well.
4. Add quinoa and cocoa nibs, stir well, divide in 9 silicon molds, then put in the fridge and leave it there for 50 minutes.
5. Serve right away!

Enjoy!

Nutritional value: 90 calories, 7 grams of fat, 8 grams of carbs, 4 grams of sugar, 2 grams of protein

# Spring Apricot Crumble
It's time you tried something different! So, try this apricot crumble!

Ingredients:
*For the oatmeal:*
3 tablespoons of buckwheat groats
1 cup of rolled oats
1 ½ tablespoons of hemp seeds
1 teaspoon of cinnamon
1 teaspoon of stevia
A pinch of salt
½ teaspoon of ginger, finely grated
2 cups of almond milk
1 teaspoon of blackstrap molasses
*For the apricots:*
1 teaspoon of stevia
1 teaspoon of cornstarch
2 cups of apricots, thinly sliced
Juice from 1 lemon

Directions:
1. In a bowl, mix oats with buckwheat groats, hemp seeds, 1 teaspoon of stevia, a pinch of salt, cinnamon, ginger, almond milk and molasses. Stir well, cover and keep in the fridge overnight.
2. In a bowl, mix apricots with 1 teaspoon of stevia, lemon juice, and cornstarch. Stir well.
3. Pour this into a greased pie pan, pour oatmeal mix on top, then put the food in the oven at 375 degrees F and bake for 30 minutes.
4. Take crumble out of the oven, leave aside for 5 minutes and then serve.

Enjoy!

Nutritional value: 230 calories, 4 grams of fat, 45 grams of carbs, 6 grams of fiber, 11 grams of sugar, 5 grams of protein

## Springs Almond and Fig Granola Parfait
It's tasty, it's perfect and very easy to make! You just have to try it!

Ingredients:
2 cups of brown rice cereal
2 cup of old-fashioned rolled oats
2 cups of Kamut, puffed
2 cups of millet, puffed
1 teaspoon of cinnamon
1 cup of almonds, thinly sliced
1 cup of dried figs cut into quarters
2 tablespoons of almond butter
½ cup of agave syrup
1 tablespoon of coconut oil, melted
Seeds from 2 vanilla beans
1 tablespoon of vanilla extract
2 blood oranges, chopped
16 ounces of coconut yogurt

Directions:
1. In a bowl, mix rice cereal with oats, Kamut, millet, almonds, and cinnamon. Stir well.
2. In another bowl, mix almond butter with agave syrup, vanilla seeds, vanilla extract and coconut oil. Stir well.
3. Combine the 2 mixtures and stir well again.
4. Pour this in 2 lined baking sheets, spread evenly, then put the food in the oven at 275 degrees F and bake for 20 minutes.
5. Take the food out of the oven, sprinkle figs on top, stir gently, then put the food in the oven again and bake for 15 more minutes.
6. Take out of the oven and divide a ¼ cup of granola into 2 dessert bowls.
7. Add ¼ cup of coconut yogurt, a few slices of orange, then top each bowl with another layer of granola, yogurt, oranges and finally a layer of granola.

Enjoy!

Nutritional value: 150 calories, 5 grams of fat, 16 grams of carbs, 3 grams of fiber, 5 grams of sugar, 3 grams of protein

# Vegan Chocolate Butter Cups
They are totally incredible and delicious!

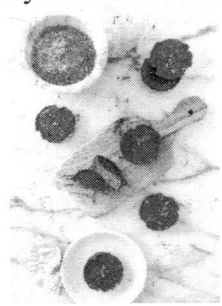

Ingredients:
5 tablespoons of almond flour
½ cup of soft coconut butter
1 cup of vegan chocolate, chopped
1 teaspoon of matcha powder + some more for the topping
3 tablespoons of palm sugar
1 teaspoon of coconut oil
A pinch of salt
Cocoa nibs

Directions:
1. In a bowl, mix coconut butter with almond flour, palm sugar, and matcha powder. Then stir, cover and keep in the fridge for 10 minutes.
2. Put vegan chocolate in a bowl and place it over another bowl filled with boiling water. Stir until it melts and mixes with coconut oil.
3. Spoon 2 teaspoons of this melted mix into a muffin liner.
4. Repeat this with 7 other muffin liners.
5. Take 1 tablespoon of matcha mix and shape a ball, place the ball in a muffin liner, press to flatten it and repeat this with the rest of the muffin liners.
6. Top each flattened ball with 1 tablespoon of melted chocolate and spread evenly.
7. In a small bowl, mix sea salt with 1/8 teaspoon of matcha powder. Stir, and sprinkle all over the muffins.
8. Add cocoa nibs on top of each, put them in the freezer and wait until they are solid.
9. Take them out of the freezer, leave at room temperature for a few minutes, then serve.

Enjoy!

Nutritional value: 230 calories, 2 grams of fat, 14 grams of carbs, 1 gram of sugar, 4 grams of sugar, 3 grams of protein

## Chapter 2. Delicious Vegan Desserts for Summer

### Summer Carrot Cake
It looks so beautiful and it tastes wonderful!

Ingredients:
*For the cashew frosting:*
2 tablespoons of lemon juice
2 cups of cashews, soaked
2 tablespoons of coconut oil, melted
1/3 cup of maple syrup
Water
*For the cake:*
1 cup of pineapple, dried and chopped
2 carrots, chopped
1 ½ cups of oat flour
1 cup of dates
½ cup of dry coconut
½ teaspoon of cinnamon

Directions:
1. In your blender, mix cashews with lemon juice, coconut oil, maple syrup and some apple. Pulse well, transfer the mix into a bowl and leave it aside.
2. Put carrots in your food processor and pulse them a few times.
3. Add flour, dates, pineapple, coconut and cinnamon, and pulse well again.
4. Pour half of this mix into a springform pan, and spread evenly.
5. Add 1/3 of the frosting and spread.
6. Add the rest of the cake mix and the rest of the frosting.
7. Put the food in the freezer and wait until it's hard enough.
8. Cut and serve.

Enjoy!

Nutritional value: 140 calories, 3 grams of fat, 23 grams of carbs, 4 grams of fiber, 5 grams of sugar, 4 grams of protein

# Salted Caramel Summer Ice Cream
It's different but amazing at the same time! You should try this vegan dessert soon!

Ingredients:
*For the caramel sauce:*
¾ cup of coconut sugar
½ cup of coconut milk
2 tablespoons of maple syrup
1 teaspoon of vanilla extract
A pinch of salt
*For the ice cream:*
12 ounces of firm tofu
1 can of coconut milk
A pinch of salt
100 drops liquid stevia
2 teaspoons of guar gum

Directions:
1. In a pan, heat up, over medium-high heat, ½ cup of coconut milk, coconut sugar, a pinch of salt and maple syrup.
2. Stir well, bring to a boil, reduce heat to low and simmer for 3-4 minutes.
3. Take off heat, add vanilla extract, stir, and leave in the fridge to cool down completely.
4. In your food processor, mix canned coconut milk, tofu, a pinch of salt and salted caramel. Pulse well.
5. Add guar gum and blend well.
6. Take mix from the fridge and transfer it into an ice cream maker.
7. When the ice cream is ready, transfer it into bowls and serve it with salted caramel on top. Enjoy!

Nutritional value: 161 calories, 7 grams of fat, 21 grams of carbs, 0 grams of fiber, 15 grams of sugar, 3 grams of protein

# Summer Passion Fruit Mousse
It can't get better than this! Such a special summer dessert!

Ingredients:
1 ½ cups of cocoa butter
1 ¼ cups of passion fruit puree
3 tablespoons of arrowroot
26 ounces of silk tofu, drained
1 ½ cups of raw sugar
A pinch of salt
½ teaspoon of vanilla extract
10 ounces of strawberries, chopped

Directions:
1. Put cocoa butter, arrowroot, and passionfruit puree in a pot, heat up over medium heat, stir, cook until butter melts, and take off heat.
2. Put tofu, a pinch of salt, vanilla and sugar in your food processor, and pulse a few times.
3. Add butter mix, and pulse again for 2 minutes.
4. Transfer this into dessert bowls or glasses, put them in the fridge and wait 4 hours.
5. Serve with chopped strawberries on top.

Enjoy!

Nutritional value: 188 calories, 10 grams of fat, 21 grams of carbs, 1 gram of fiber, 15 grams of sugar, 3 grams of protein

# Vegan Sesame and Ginger Ice Cream
A hot summer day can only improve with a tasty ice cream! Try this vegan one!

Ingredients:
4 dates, pitted
1 banana
3 tablespoons of hemp seeds
1 ½ cup of water
1 ½ cup of coconut milk
½ cup of black sesame seeds
¼ teaspoon of vanilla
1 inch of ginger
1 persimmon, thinly sliced for serving

Directions:
1. Put sesame seeds in your coffee grinder, crush them well and then transfer them to your kitchen blender.
2. Add banana, ginger, dates, hemp seeds, water, vanilla and coconut milk, and mix well until it's creamy enough.
3. Transfer the mix into a container, keep it in the freezer for 6 hours and then put it in dessert bowls.
4. Serve with sliced persimmon on top.

Enjoy!

Nutritional value: 132 calories, 7 grams of fat, 14 grams of carbs, 0 grams of fiber, 12 grams of sugar, 2 grams of protein

# Delicious Vegan Chia Seeds Pudding
It's a very fresh and tasty vegan summer dessert!

Ingredients:
1 cup of almond milk
½ cup of pumpkin puree
2 tablespoons of maple syrup
½ cup of coconut milk
½ teaspoon of cinnamon
½ teaspoon of vanilla extract
¼ teaspoon of ginger finely grated
¼ cup of chia seeds

Directions:
1. In a bowl, mix almond milk with coconut milk, pumpkin puree, cinnamon, maple syrup, vanilla, and ginger. Stir well.
2. Add chia seeds, stir, and leave aside for 20 minutes.
3. Spoon into 4 glasses, cover and keep in the fridge for 1 hour.

Enjoy!

Nutritional value: 135 calories, 7 grams of fat, 10 grams of carbs, 10 grams of fiber, 6 grams of protein

## Summer Mango and Coconut Sorbet
It's one of our favorite vegan summer desserts!

Ingredients:
3 cups of mango, cut into medium chunks
½ cup of light coconut milk
¼ cup of raw sugar

Directions:
1. Put mango pieces in your blender, and pulse a few times.
2. Add sugar, and pulse some more.
3. Add coconut milk at the end, blend for 15 seconds, transfer to bowls and serve right away or keep in the freezer for 20 minutes if you want a firmer sorbet.

Enjoy!

Nutritional value: 160 calories, 2 grams of fat, 38 grams of carbs, 2 grams of fiber, 1 gram of protein

## Vegan Chocolate Sorbet
We thought that you might like this amazing vegan sorbet! Try it in the summer!

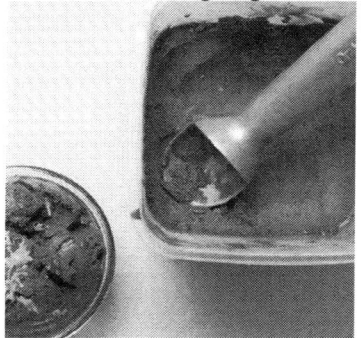

Ingredients:
2 cups of water
1/3 cup of raw brown sugar
2/3 cup of raw white sugar
A pinch of salt
¾ cup of cocoa powder
6 ounces of vegan dark chocolate, chopped
Zest and juice from 1 lemon

Directions:
1. Put 1 ½ cups of water in a pot and heat it up over medium heat.
2. Add brown and white sugar, a pinch of salt and cocoa powder. Stir, bring to a boil and simmer for 1 minutes until everything melts.
3. Take pot off the heat, add chocolate, and stir until it melts.
4. Add the rest of the water, lemon zest, and juice, and stir again well.
5. Leave the mix aside to completely cool down, then transfer it into your ice cream maker and turn it on.
6. Put the mix into bowls, and serve when you're ready!
Enjoy!

Nutritional value: 160 calories, 8 grams of fat, 35 grams of carbs, 21 grams of fiber, 1 gram of sugar, 12 grams of protein

# Amazing Vegan Summer Dessert
## Discover a unique vegan dessert!

Ingredients:
4 cups of cherries, sliced in half
2 teaspoons of coconut oil
2 cups of walnuts, cut into pieces and soaked for 30 minutes
1 vanilla bean
Coconut sugar to taste
2 tablespoons of almond milk as needed

Directions:
1. Heat up a grill pan with the coconut oil over medium-high heat, add cherries, grill them for a few minutes, flip them with a spatula and cook them for another few minutes, remove them from heat and leave aside.
2. Put walnuts in your food processor, add vanilla seeds, almond milk, and coconut sugar to taste, and blend very well.
3. Transfer cherries into dessert bowls and serve them with the walnut cream you've made.

Enjoy!

Nutritional value: 110 calories, 2 grams of fat, 19 grams of carbs, 0 grams of fiber, 15 grams of sugar, 3 grams of protein

# Pineapple Upside Down Cake
It's going to be one of your favorite summer desserts!

Ingredients:
3 cups of white flour
¼ cup of grape seed oil
1 cup of vegan butter + ½ cup of melted vegan butter
1 teaspoon of vanilla extract
2 ¼ cups of white vegan sugar
1 ¼ cup of applesauce
2 teaspoons of baking powder
1 ¼ cups of soy milk
2 tablespoons of white vinegar
1 ½ cups of vegan brown sugar
16 pecans
16 pineapple slices

Directions:
1. Grease 2 cake pans with grape seed oil, sprinkle some flour, and coat well.
2. Sprinkle brown sugar, and coat as well. Pour ½ cup of melted vegan butter, and spread evenly.
3. Put 1 pineapple slice in the middle of each pan. Add the rest of the slices in a circle around the edges of the cake pans.
4. Add 1 pecan in the middle of each pineapple slice. Leave pans aside for now.
5. In a bowl, mix soy milk with white vinegar. Stir, and leave aside as well.
6. In another bowl, add the rest of the butter, and mix using your hand mixer for a few seconds.
7. Add the white sugar, and mix again. Add vanilla and applesauce, and stir again well.
8. In a bowl, mix flour with a pinch of salt and baking powder.
9. Add this mix to the soy milk mix, and stir well. Pour the mix over pineapples. Spread, then put the pans in the oven at 350 degrees F and bake for 40 minutes.
10. Take cakes out of the oven, leave them aside for 10 minutes, invert them on platters and cut when they are cold enough.

Enjoy!

Nutritional value: 200 calories, 10 grams of fat, 23 grams of carbs, 1 gram of fiber, 4 grams of protein

# Vegan Summer Cake
## A very tasty vegan cake with such a creamy filling!

Ingredients:
¼ cup of coconut oil, already melted
1 cup of quinoa
¼ cup of coconut sugar
*For the mint layer:*
1 cup of raw cashews, soaked for 3 hours, drained and rinsed
½ cup of water
1 tablespoon of lemon juice
1/6 cup of mint, roughly chopped
1/6 cup of coconut sugar
2 teaspoons of spirulina powder
1 tablespoon of coconut oil
2 tablespoons of chia seeds
*For the vanilla layer:*
1 and 1/6 cups of cashews, soaked for 3 hours, drained and rinsed
1 tablespoon of lemon juice
½ cup of water
1 tablespoon of coconut oil
1/6 cup of coconut sugar
1 teaspoon of vanilla extract
2 tablespoons of chia seeds

*For the pink layer:*
½ cup of water
1 cup of cashews, soaked for 3 hours, drained and rinsed
1 tablespoon of lemon juice
1 tablespoon of coconut oil
1/6 cup of coconut sugar
2 tablespoons of chia seeds
¼ cup of red beet, thinly sliced

Directions:
1. Put quinoa in your kitchen blender, and pulse a few times.

1. Transfer the paste into a bowl and mix it with ¼ cup of coconut oil (already melted) and ¼ cup of coconut sugar. Stir well.
2. Transfer the mix to a cake pan, press on the bottom evenly, and keep in the fridge.
3. In your blender, mix 1 cup of cashews with ½ cup of water, 1 tablespoon of lemon juice, 1/6 cup of coconut sugar, 1/6 cup of mint, 2 teaspoons of spirulina, 1 tablespoon of coconut oil, and pulse until it blends.
4. Add 2 tablespoons of chia seeds, blend well, transfer the mix into a bowl, leave aside and clean your blender.
5. Put 1 1/6 cups of cashews in the blender and mix it with ½ cup of water, 1 tablespoon of lemon juice, 1/6 cup of coconut sugar, 1 tablespoon of coconut oil and 1 teaspoon of vanilla extract.
6. Blend well. Add 2 tablespoons of chia seeds, pulse a few more times, transfer the mix into a bowl and clean the blender again.
7. Add 1 cup of cashews to your blender and mix it with ½ cup of water, 1 tablespoon of lemon juice, 1/6 cup of coconut sugar, 1 tablespoon of coconut oil ¼ cup of red beet.
8. Blend well. Add 2 tablespoons of chia seeds, and pulse a few more times.
9. Take cake crust out of the fridge and spread the mint layer evenly all over it.
10. Add the vanilla layer over the mint one. Spread evenly.
11. Add the red beet layer at the end, spread evenly, and put the cake in the fridge and wait 1 day.
12. Take it out of the fridge, leave aside for 30 minutes, cut and serve it.
Enjoy!

Nutritional value: 370 calories, 8 grams of fat, 40 grams of carbs, 1 gram of fiber, 14 grams of sugar, 3 grams of protein

# Summer Lemon Fudge
Sit back and enjoy!

Ingredients:
1/3 cup of natural cashew butter
1 ½ tablespoons of soft coconut oil
2 tablespoons of coconut butter
5 tablespoons of lemon juice
½ teaspoon of lemon zest
A pinch of salt
1 tablespoon of maple syrup

Directions:
1. In a bowl, mix cashew butter with coconut one, coconut oil, lemon juice, lemon zest, a pinch of salt and maple syrup. Stir until you obtain a creamy mix.
2. Line a muffin tray with some parchment paper. Scoop 1 tablespoon of lemon fudge mix into each of the 10 pieces, then put it in the freezer and keep it there for a few hours.
3. Take the food out of the fridge and wait 20 minutes before you serve them.
Enjoy!

Nutritional value: 72 calories, 4 grams of fat, 8 grams of carbs, 0 grams of fiber, 2 grams of sugar, 1 gram of protein

# Summer Raw Fudge
It's another delicious fudge idea!

Ingredients:
¼ cup of cocoa powder
1 cup of cashew butter
A pinch of salt
1/3 cup of coconut oil
¼ cup of maple syrup
1 teaspoon of vanilla extract

Directions:
1. In a bowl, mix coconut oil with the butter, and stir well.
2. Add cocoa powder, maple syrup, a pinch of salt and the vanilla. Stir until the mix is creamy.
3. Pour this into a dish lined with some plastic foil, then put it in the freezer and wait a few hours.
4. Take fudge out of the freezer and wait 1 hour before slicing it and serving it.

Enjoy!

Nutritional value: 68 calories, 0 grams of fat, 15 grams of carbs, 0 grams of fiber, 14 grams of sugar, 0 grams of protein

# Summer Tahini Dessert
When you'll taste this dessert, you will fall in love with it!

Ingredients:
4 dates, soaked and drained
½ cup of cocoa powder
¾ cup of tahini
½ teaspoon of vanilla powder
1/3 cup of melted coconut oil
A pinch of salt
Sesame seeds for serving

Directions:
1. Put dates in your food processor, and pulse a few times.
2. Add tahini, and pulse again until you obtain a puree.
3. Add cocoa powder, a pinch of salt, coconut oil, and vanilla extract, and pulse well.
4. Pour this into a greased loaf pan, then put it in the freezer and keep it there for 4 hours.
5. Take the food out of the freezer, sprinkle sesame seeds on top, leave at room temperature for 30 minutes, cut, arrange on a serving platter, and serve.

Enjoy!

Nutritional value: 120, calories, 12 grams of fat, 4 grams of carbs, 1 gram of fiber, 0 grams of sugar, 2 grams of protein

## Delicious Vegan Raspberry Truffles
A great dessert for a fancy summer party!

Ingredients:
½ an avocado flesh
6 ounces of vegan chocolate, melted
A pinch of salt
2 tablespoons of raspberry liqueur
20 frozen raspberries

Directions:
1. Put avocado in a bowl and mash it well.
2. Add a pinch of salt, vegan chocolate, and stir well.
3. Add liqueur, and stir well.
4. Put everything in the fridge for 40 minutes.
5. Put raspberries in a bowl and mash them well.
6. Take the mix from the fridge, shape small balls, and roll them in raspberry puree.
7. Arrange them on a plate and serve right away!

Enjoy!

Nutritional value: 70 calories, 3 grams of fat, 3 grams of carbs, 0 grams of fiber, 1 gram of sugar, 1 gram of protein

# Vegan Summer Pops
They're so easy to make and taste so good. Kids are going to love them!

Ingredients:
10 kiwis
2 teaspoons of coconut milk
1 cup of vegan chocolate, melted
Coconut flakes
Chopped nuts for serving

Directions:
1. Slice kiwis ½ an inch thick.
2. Insert stick in each kiwi slice, arrange them on lined baking sheet and keep them in your freezer for 30 minutes.
3. Put vegan chocolate in a pot and heat it up over medium heat.
4. Add coconut oil. Stir and cook for 20 seconds.
5. Dip kiwi pops in this mix, arrange them on the baking sheet again, sprinkle coconut flakes and chopped nuts all over, then put the pops in the fridge and keep them there until they're ready to be served.

Enjoy!

Nutritional value: 78 calories, 5 grams of fat, 7 grams of carbs, 0 grams of fiber, 5 grams of sugar, 0 grams of protein

## Tasty Summer Avocado Truffles
### It's delicious!

Ingredients:
2 avocados, pitted
1 ½ cups of vegan chocolate chips
1 teaspoon of vanilla extract
½ cup of coconut, shredded
A pinch of salt

Directions:
1. Put avocados in your blender, pulse well, and leave aside for now.
2. Put chocolate chips in a bowl, then put them in your microwave and melt them for 40 seconds.
3. Add avocado to chocolate mix, and stir well.
4. Add a pinch of salt and vanilla extract, stir again then put the mix in the fridge and wait 2 hours.
5. Take mix out of the fridge, roll small truffles out of it, roll them in shredded coconut, arrange them on a platter, and serve.

Enjoy!

Nutritional value: 70 calories, 4 grams of fat, 6 grams of carbs, 2 grams of fiber, 4 grams of sugar, 1 gram of protein

# Summer Vegan Bars
## They will give you so much energy!

Ingredients:
¼ cup of cocoa nibs
1 cup of almonds, soaked for at least 3 hours
2 tablespoons of cocoa powder
¼ cup of hemp seeds
¼ cup of goji berries
¼ cup of coconut, shredded
A pinch of salt
8 dates, pitted and soaked

Directions:
1. Put the almonds in your food processor and blend them well.
2. Add hemp seeds, cocoa nibs, cocoa powder, goji, coconut and a pinch of salt. Blend well.
3. Gradually add dates, and blend some more.
4. Transfer mix to a parchment paper, spread and press it.
5. Place in the fridge for 30 minutes.
6. Cut in equal pieces and serve them.

Enjoy!

Nutritional value: 140 calories, 6 grams of fat, 12 grams of carbs, 3 grams of fiber, 19 grams of protein

# Vegan Chocolate Cookie Dough Bites
You are going to eat these so fast …

Ingredients:
¼ cup of vegan mini chocolate chips
1 cup of oat flour
2 tablespoons of water
¼ cup of maple syrup
1/3 cup of almond butter
1 teaspoon of vanilla
A pinch of salt
*For the chocolate shell:*
2 tablespoons of coconut oil
¼ cup of vegan chocolate chips

Directions:
1. Put flour in a bowl.
2. Add ¼ cup of vegan chocolate chips, maple syrup, almond butter, water, vanilla and a pinch of salt. Stir well.
3. Scoop a teaspoon of batter, shape a small ball and arrange the balls on a platter.
4. Repeat this with the rest of the dough. You should obtain about 100 small balls.
5. Put ¼ of the vegan chocolate chips in a pan and melt it over medium heat.
6. Add coconut oil, stir well, and take off heat.
7. Dip each ball in this mix, arrange the balls on a lined baking sheet, then put the balls in the freezer and wait 10 minutes. Then serve.

Enjoy!

Nutritional value: 122 calories, 8 grams of fat, 3 grams of carbs, 0 grams of fiber, 5 grams of sugar, 3 grams of protein

# Simple Vegan Summer Tart

What can be more delicious on a summer day than a fresh vegan tart?

Ingredients:
*For the crust:*
2 cups of graham cracker crumbs
7 tablespoons of coconut oil
*For the filling:*
¼ cup of maple syrup
2 cans of coconut milk
Zest from 1 lemon
Juice from 1 lemon
*For the topping:*
½ pint blueberries
½ pint cherries
1-pint strawberries, cut into halves

Directions:
1. Put crackers in your blender. Pulse a few times.
2. Put coconut oil in a pan, heat it up over medium-high heat, melt it and then mix it with crumbled graham crackers.
3. Put the mix into a tart pan, press well on the bottom, then put the food in the oven at 350 degrees F and bake for 10 minutes.
4. Put coconut milk in a bowl and mix it with maple syrup, lemon zest, and lemon juice. Stir well.
5. Take tart crust out of the oven, leave aside to completely cool down, pour this coconut milk mix into it, spread evenly and then put the tart in the freezer and wait 2 hours.
6. Take the tart out of the freezer, spread all the berries on top, and keep it in the fridge until you serve it.

Enjoy!

Nutritional value: 130 calories, 4 grams of fat, 10 grams of carbs, 1 gram of fiber, 4 grams of sugar, 13 grams of protein

# Vegan Frozen Banana Popsicles
They are so amazing!

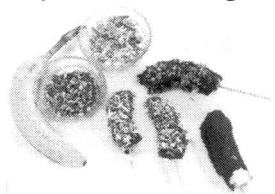

Ingredients:
10 ounces of vegan chocolate cut in chunks
1 tablespoon of coconut oil
1 teaspoon of vanilla extract
3 bananas
Some chopped nuts for serving
Toasted coconut for serving

Directions:
1. Put coconut oil in a pan and heat it up over medium heat.
2. Add vanilla and vegan chocolate. Stir, and leave the stove on until everything melts.
3. Take this mix off heat and leave it aside to melt.
4. Cut each banana in half, stick a skewer in each, dip them in chocolate mix and arrange them on a lined baking sheet.
5. Sprinkle nuts and toasted coconut over them, then put them in the freezer and keep them there for 40 minutes.
6. Serve them when they are frozen enough.

Enjoy!

Nutritional value: 160 calories, 6 grams of fat, 25 grams of carbs, 2 grams of fiber, 14 grams of sugar

# Vegan Twinkies with Tasty Coconut Filling
They have the word "summer" written all over!

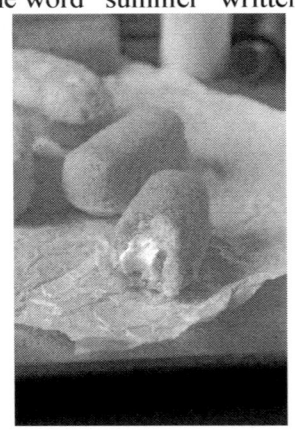

Ingredients:
*For the cake:*
1 ½ teaspoons of baking powder
1 cup of all-purpose flour
½ cup of raw sugar
A pinch of salt
3 tablespoons of coconut oil
1 teaspoon of apple cider vinegar
1 teaspoon of vanilla extract
1 teaspoon of baking soda
½ cup of almond milk
*For the coconut filling:*
1 can of coconut milk
½ cup of powdered sugar
2 teaspoons of vanilla extract

Directions:
1. In a bowl, mix the flour with a pinch of salt, baking powder, and soda. Stir, and leave aside.
2. In another bowl, mix the vanilla extract with raw sugar and coconut oil. Stir well.
3. Add flour mix, almond milk, cider vinegar, and stir again using your mixer.
4. Pour this mix into a greased pan, spread, then put it in the oven at 350 degrees F and bake for 20 minutes.
5. Take the food out of the oven and leave it aside to completely cool down. Cut them.
6. Put cold coconut milk in a bowl and stir using your hand mixer until it's fluffy enough.
7. Add powdered sugar and vanilla, stir again and then put the food in the fridge.
8. Put coconut cream in a squeeze bottle, make 5 holes in each Twinkie, fill them half through and keep them in the fridge until you serve them.

Enjoy!

Nutritional value: 150 calories, 10 grams of fat, 30 grams of carbs, 0 grams of fiber, 24 grams of sugar 4

# Tasty Vegan Root Beer Cupcakes
It's smooth, it's fresh, it's a root beer cupcake!

Ingredients:
1 cup of root beer soda
¾ cup of raw sugar
1 teaspoon of apple cider vinegar
1/3 cup of canola oil
2 teaspoons of root beer extract
½ teaspoon of vanilla extract
1 and 1/3 cups of all-purpose flour
¾ teaspoon of baking soda
½ teaspoon of baking powder

Directions:
1. Put root beer soda in your kitchen blender.
2. Add vinegar, and pulse a few times.
3. Add sugar, oil, root beer extract, vanilla extract, flour, baking powder, and soda. Blend until you obtain a smooth batter.
4. Pour this into a lined muffin tray, then put it in the oven at 350 degrees F and bake for 15 minutes.
5. Take muffins out of the oven, leave aside to cool down, transfer to serving platter, and serve. Enjoy!

Nutritional value: 98 calories, 6 grams of fat, 7 grams of carbs, 0 grams of fiber, 6 grams of sugar, 1 gram of protein

# Vegan Almond Bundt Cake
Get ready for one of the most delicious and amazing vegan summer desserts!

Ingredients:
¼ cup of gluten-free flour
¼ teaspoon of baking powder
¼ teaspoon of baking soda
A pinch of salt
1 tablespoon of warm coconut oil
¼ cup of dates, pitted and soaked for 30 minutes
¼ cup of dates water, reserved
½ teaspoon of vanilla extract
½ teaspoon of almond extract
½ tablespoon of cider vinegar
¼ cup of coconut milk
Some powdered sugar for serving

Directions:
1. Grease 2 Bundt pans and leave them aside for now.
2. In a bowl, mix the flour with a pinch of salt, baking powder, and soda. Stir.
3. In another bowl, mix the coconut oil with dates, reserved water, vanilla extract, almond extract, cider vinegar and coconut milk. Stir well.
4. Mix flour with wet ingredients, stir well to combine, pour into greased pans, then put the food in the oven at 375 degrees F and bake for 20 minutes.
5. Take cakes out of the oven, leave aside to cool down, transfer them into platters, and serve with powdered sugar sprinkled on top.

Enjoy!

Nutritional value: 270 calories, 15 grams of fat, 29 grams of carbs, 2 grams of fiber, 15 grams of sugar, 5 grams of protein

# Vegan Tangerine Cake
## It has a perfectly balanced taste and flavor!

Ingredients:
¾ cup of raw sugar
2 cups of all-purpose flour
¼ cup of canola oil
½ cup of coconut milk
1 teaspoon of cider vinegar
½ teaspoon of vanilla extract
Juice and zest of 2 lemons
Juice and zest from 1 tangerine
Tangerine segments for serving

Directions:
1. Put flour in a bowl, mix with salt and sugar, and leave aside.
2. In another bowl, mix oil with coconut milk, vinegar, vanilla extract, lemon juice and zest and zest from the tangerine. Stir well.
3. Mix flour with wet ingredients. Stir until you obtain a batter, pour the batter into a greased cake pan, then put it in the oven at 375 degrees F and bake for 20 minutes.
4. Take cake out of the oven, leave aside to cool down, transfer it to a platter, then cut and pour the tangerine juice all over it.
5. Serve right away with tangerine segments on top.

Enjoy!

Nutritional value: 190 calories, 1 gram of fat, 20 grams of carbs, 0 grams of fiber, 12 grams of sugar, 2 grams of protein

# Vegan Summer Cupcakes
These are the best vegan cupcakes!

Ingredients:
1 and 1/3 cup of whole wheat flour
2 tablespoons of flax seeds + 6 tablespoons of water
½ teaspoon of cinnamon
½ teaspoon of baking soda
1 teaspoon of baking powder
¼ teaspoon of grated ginger
½ cup of extra virgin olive oil
¼ teaspoon of nutmeg
2 tablespoons of soy milk
¾ cup of coconut sugar
1 teaspoon of vanilla extract
2/3 cup of carrot, finely grated

Directions:
1. Put flax seeds and water in your kitchen blender. Pulse well.
2. In a bowl, mix flour with baking soda and powder, ginger, cinnamon and nutmeg. Stir well.
3. In another bowl, mix blended flax seeds with sugar, oil, milk, carrot, and vanilla extract. Stir well.
4. Mix flour with wet ingredients, and stir well.
5. Pour batter into a lined muffin pan, then put it in the oven at 320 degrees F and bake them for 25 minutes.
6. Take muffins out of the oven, leave them to cool down, then transfer them to a platter, and serve. Enjoy!

Nutritional value: 224 calories, 11 grams of fat, 27 grams of carbs, 12 grams of sugar, 1 gram of fiber, 2 grams of protein

# Chapter 3. Delicious Autumn Vegan Desserts

## Pumpkin and Quinoa Cookies
You'll ask for more!

Ingredients:
1 cup of quinoa flakes
1 tablespoon of tapioca starch
1 cup of brown rice flour
¼ cup of millet flour
A pinch of salt
1 teaspoon of xanthan gum
1 teaspoon of baking soda
1 teaspoon of cinnamon
1 ¼ cup of light brown sugar
½ teaspoon of nutmeg
¼ teaspoon of cloves
½ cup of coconut oil
1 cup of canned pumpkin
1 tablespoon of maple syrup
1 tablespoon of vanilla extract
¼ teaspoon of lemon juice
½ cup of raisins
1 cup of vegan chocolate chips
½ cup of nuts, chopped

Directions:
1. In a bowl, mix quinoa flakes with rice flour, millet flour, tapioca starch, xanthan gum, a pinch of salt, baking soda, brown sugar, cinnamon, nutmeg, and cloves. Stir well.
2. Add coconut oil, and stir well. Then, add pumpkin, vanilla extract, maple syrup and lemon juice. Stir well. Add chocolate chips, raisins and nuts. Stir.
3. Scoop spoonfuls of dough on a lined baking sheet, then put the cookies in the oven and bake at 350 degrees F for 20 minutes.
4. Take cookies out of the oven, then transfer them onto a plate, and serve them.

Nutritional value: 75 calories, 3 grams of fat, 9 grams of carbs, 1 gram of fiber, 4 grams of sugar, 1 gram of protein

# Delicious Vegan Apple Cake
It's a great autumn dessert and it's completely gluten-free!

Ingredients:
1 banana
½ cup of dates
½ cup of almonds
½ cup of cashews
2 tablespoons of agave
1 teaspoon of vanilla
1 cup of almond milk
½ cup of coconut oil
1 cup of roasted applesauce
½ cup of coconut flour
½ cup of rice flour
2 tablespoons potato starch
1 ½ tablespoons baking powder
1 tablespoon of xanthan gum
A pinch of salt
1 teaspoon of baking soda
¼ teaspoon of cinnamon
A pinch of nutmeg
3 apples, chopped
Juice from 1 lemon
Dried cranberries for garnishing

Directions:
1. In your kitchen blender, mix cashews with almonds, then pulse a few times and transfer the mix into a bowl.
2. Mix this with rice flour, coconut flour, potato starch, xanthan gum, baking powder and soda, a pinch of salt and cinnamon.
3. Meanwhile, in a food processor, mix banana with vanilla, dates, agave, almond milk and coconut oil. Blend well.
4. Add this to the dry mix and stir well until you obtain a batter.
5. Put chopped apples in a bowl and mix with half of the lemon juice.
6. Add these to the batter, and stir well.
7. Also, add the rest of the lemon juice and a pinch of nutmeg. Stir.

8. Pour this into a greased baking pan, spread evenly, then put the food in the oven at 350 degrees F and bake for 25 minutes.
9. Take cake out of the oven, leave aside for a few minutes, cut, arrange on plates, top with roasted applesauce and cranberries. Then serve.

Enjoy!

Nutritional value: 175 calories, 5 grams of fat, 30 grams of carbs, 3 grams of fiber, 15 grams of sugar, 4 grams of protein

# Apple and Maple Crisp
## It's worth all your admiration!

Ingredients:
6 apples, thinly sliced
2 tablespoons of pure maple syrup
1 tablespoon of lemon juice
2 teaspoons of tapioca
¾ cup of sorghum flour
1 cup of quinoa flakes
1 cup of light brown sugar
1 teaspoon of ginger, finely grated
2 teaspoons of cinnamon
A pinch of salt
¾ cup of organic coconut oil

Directions:
1. Put apples in a bowl, add lemon juice and toss to coat.
2. Add maple syrup and tapioca starch. Stir again.
3. Transfer these to a greased baking dish, and spread evenly.
4. In a bowl, mix quinoa flakes with rice flour, cinnamon, salt, and ginger. Stir well.
5. Add coconut oil and blend well.
6. Pour this over the apple slices, spread, then put the food in the oven at 350 degrees F and bake for 20 minutes.
7. Take out of the oven, cover with a tin foil, then put it in the oven again and bake for 20 more minutes.
8. Leave crisp to cool down. Cut and serve.
Enjoy!

Nutritional value: 191 calories, 6 grams of fat, 33 grams of carbs, 3 grams of fiber, 2 grams of protein, 5 grams of sugar

# Amazing Vegan Gingerbread Cake
A vegan dessert for autumn!

Ingredients:
6 tablespoons of warm water
2 tablespoons of flax seeds
5/6 cup of teff flour
5/6 cup of millet flour
1 teaspoon of baking powder
1/3 cup of potato starch
2 teaspoons of ginger, finely ground
1 teaspoon of baking soda
¼ teaspoon of cloves
1 teaspoon of cinnamon
A pinch of salt
2/3 cup of coconut palm sugar
½ cup of molasses
1 cup of applesauce
1/3 cup of coconut oil

Directions:
1. In a bowl, mix flax seeds with water. Stir, cover and leave aside for 10 minutes.
2. Meanwhile, in a bowl, mix millet and teff flour with potato starch, baking powder, baking soda, ginger, cinnamon, cloves and a pinch of salt. Stir well.
3. In another bowl, mix palm sugar with molasses, coconut oil, and applesauce. Stir well.
4. Combine dry and wet ingredients. Stir, then pour the mix into a greased pan and put it in the oven at 350 degrees F and bake for 35 minutes.
5. Take out of the oven, leave aside to cool down, and eat on the second day.
Enjoy!

Nutritional value: 271 calories, 8 grams of fat, 48 grams of carbs, 2 grams of fiber, 27 grams of sugar, 2 grams of protein

# Vegan Pumpkin Bread
It's a rich vegan dessert for a cold autumn day!

Ingredients:
1 tablespoon of cinnamon
1 cup of pumpkin puree
1 cup of buckwheat flour
¼ teaspoon of cloves
¼ teaspoon of ground ginger
¼ cup of coconut oil
¼ cup of water
1 teaspoon of vanilla
6 tablespoons of maple syrup
1 tablespoon of apple cider vinegar
1 teaspoon of baking soda

Directions:
1. In a bowl, mix buckwheat flour with ginger, cinnamon, baking soda and cloves. Stir well.
2. Add coconut oil, pumpkin puree, maple syrup, water and vanilla. Stir everything.
3. Add cider vinegar. Stir, then pour the mix into a lined loaf pan and put it in the oven at 350 degrees F and bake for 1 hour.
4. Take bread out of the oven, leave aside to cool down, cut and serve.

Enjoy!

Nutritional value: 165 calories, 10 grams of fat, 14 grams of carbs, 4 grams of fiber, 6 grams of sugar, 5 grams of protein

# Vegan Apricot Muffins
It's a simple and delicious autumn dessert!

Ingredients:
½ cup of bread flour
1 ½ cup of whole wheat flour
A pinch of salt
1 ½ teaspoon of baking powder
1 teaspoon of baking soda
1 teaspoon of cinnamon
1 tablespoon of flax seeds, mixed with 3 tablespoons of water
¼ cup of agave syrup
½ cup of brown rice syrup
¼ cup of canola oil
¾ cup of almond milk
½ cup of almonds, finely chopped
1 cup of apricots, dried and blended in your food processor

Directions:
1. In a bowl, mix whole wheat flour with bread flour, baking powder and soda, salt, cinnamon and flax seeds. Stir.
2. In another bowl, mix rice syrup with agave syrup, almond milk, canola oil, apricots, and almonds. Stir again.
3. Mix wet and dry ingredients. Stir until you obtain a smooth batter, then pour the mix into a lined 12-piece muffin tray and put it in the oven 425 degrees F and bake for 20 minutes.
4. Take muffins out of the oven, leave aside for 10 minutes, then transfer the muffins to a platter and serve.
   Enjoy!

Nutritional value: 168 calories, 7 grams of fat, 23 grams of carbs, 1 gram of fiber, 3 grams of sugar, 2 grams of protein

# Apple and Nut Tart
A creamy, fruity, autumn dessert!

Ingredients:
1 cup of blanched almond flour
1 cup of quinoa flour
1 cup of oat flour
A pinch of salt
½ teaspoon of pumpkin pie spice
1 drop vanilla stevia
1 tablespoon of melted coconut oil
1 teaspoon of vanilla extract
½ cup of coconut milk
¼ cup of apple juice
*For the topping:*
¼ cup of raspberry jam
Some lemon juice
1 apple, thinly sliced
A handful of pine nuts

Directions:
1. In a bowl, mix all flours with pumpkin pie spice and a pinch of salt.
2. Add some of the coconut oil, stevia, vanilla, apple juice and coconut milk, and mix using your hands until you obtain a sticky dough.
3. Transfer this to a floured working surface, knead for a few minutes, shape into balls, press, and roll them, then transfer the balls onto a lined baking pan. Add jam, and spread it.
4. Also, add apples and nuts, brush them with the rest of the coconut oil, then put the tart in the oven at 350 degrees F and bake for 20 minutes.
5. Take out of the oven and serve only when it's warm.

Enjoy!

Nutritional value: 212 calories, 9 grams of fat, 32 grams of carbs, 3 grams of fiber, 13 grams of sugar, 1 gram of protein

# Apple and Cider Bread
It's not only a dessert - it could also be a perfect autumn dinner!

Ingredients:
¼ cup of tapioca flour
½ cup of quinoa flour
2 cups of sorghum flour
4 teaspoons of baking powder
¼ cup of arrowroot flour
1 tablespoon of cane sugar
2 teaspoons of xanthan gum
1 ¾ cup of pure apple cider
A pinch of salt
1 tablespoon of extra virgin olive oil

Directions:
1. In a bowl, combine tapioca flour with quinoa flour, sorghum flour, arrowroot flour, cane sugar, a pinch of salt, xanthan gum and baking powder. Whisk.
2. Add cider, and stir until you obtain a batter.
3. Pour this into a greased loaf pan, spread, brush with the olive oil, then put the food in the oven at 375 degrees F and bake for 1 hour.
4. Take the bread out of the oven, leave aside for 40 minutes, cut and serve.

Enjoy!

Nutritional value: 179 calories, 1 gram of fat, 42 grams of carbs, 3 grams of fiber, 21 grams of sugar, 3 grams of protein

# Autumn Pumpkin and Pecan Granola
Nutritious and delicious granola!

Ingredients:
2/3 cups of almonds, finely chopped
3 cups of pecans, finely chopped
5 cups of rolled oats
A pinch of salt
1 tablespoon of pumpkin pie spice
1/3 cup of flax seeds
2/3 cup of maple syrup
¾ cup of pumpkin puree
2 teaspoons of vanilla extract
2 tablespoons of coconut oil
2 cups of cranberries

Directions:
1. In a bowl, mix oats with almonds, nuts, flax seeds, salt, and pumpkin pie spice. Stir.
2. In another bowl, mix pumpkin puree with coconut oil, maple syrup, and vanilla extract. Stir well.
3. Combine the 2 mixtures, stir, divide between 2 lined baking sheets, then put the food in the oven at 300 degrees F and bake for 1 hour, tossing it half way through.
4. Take granola out of the oven, leave aside to cool down, add cranberries, toss to coat, and serve.

Enjoy!

Nutritional value: 230 calories, 10 grams of fat, 32 grams of carbs, 2 grams of fiber, 12 grams of sugar, 3 grams of protein

## Vegan Pecan Scones
A fresh dessert for you to enjoy with your loved ones in the fall!

Ingredients:
1 cup of pecans
2 cups of whole wheat flour
1 teaspoon of cinnamon
1 tablespoon of baking powder
A pinch of salt
½ teaspoon of ginger, finely grated
1/3 cup of coconut oil
¾ cup of medium banana
¼ cup of almond milk
½ teaspoon of vanilla extract
2 tablespoons of maple syrup

Directions:
1. Spread evenly the nuts on a baking sheet, put them in the oven at 450 degrees F and toast for 3 minutes.
2. Take them out of the oven, leave them aside to cool down, chop, and put them in a bowl.
3. Add flour, cinnamon, baking powder, salt, and ginger. Stir well.
4. Add coconut oil and mix well.
5. In a bowl, add banana, milk, maple syrup and vanilla extract. Stir well.
6. Pour this over the flour mix and stir it until you obtain a dough.
7. Transfer dough to a floured working surface, knead it for a few minutes, shape a circle, cut it into 8 slices and arrange them on a lined baking sheet.
8. Put the slices in the oven at 375 degrees F and bake them for 17 minutes.
9. Take the slices out of the oven, leave them aside to cool down, transfer them to a platter, and serve.

Enjoy!

Nutritional value: 450 calories, 29 grams of fat, 2 grams of fiber, 43 grams of carbs, 32 grams of sugar, 6 grams of protein

# Vegan Pumpkin Spice Donuts
Irresistible vegan donuts!

Ingredients:
1 ¼ cup of white flour
1 teaspoon of baking powder
2 teaspoons of pumpkin pie spice
A pinch of salt
½ cup of almond milk
½ cup of brown sugar
1/3 cup of pumpkin puree
2 tablespoons of melted coconut oil
1 teaspoon of vanilla
¼ cup of vegan butter
1 tablespoon of cinnamon
1 cup of raw sugar

Directions:
1. In a bowl, mix flour with spice, a pinch of salt and baking powder. Stir.
2. In another bowl, mix brown sugar with pumpkin puree, almond milk, coconut oil and vanilla. Stir.
3. Combine the 2 mixtures, stirring well.
4. Spoon the batter into a donut pan, distribute evenly, then put the batter in the oven at 350 degrees F and bake for 12 minutes.
5. Meanwhile, put the vegan butter in a bowl and stir it well.
6. In another bowl, mix 1 cup of sugar with 1 tablespoon of cinnamon.
7. Take donuts out of the oven, leave them aside for a few minutes, dip them one side in butter, then in the sugar and cinnamon mix. Arrange them on a platter, and serve.

Enjoy!

Nutritional value: 230 calories, 10 grams of fat, 1 gram of fiber, 30 grams of carbs, 12 grams of sugar, 4 grams of protein

# Vegan Chocolate and Chickpea Blondies
## Something new and creative!

Ingredients:
1 ½ cups of canned chickpeas, drained and rinsed
1/8 teaspoon of baking soda
A pinch of salt
¾ teaspoon of baking powder
¾ cup of coconut sugar
2 teaspoons of vanilla extract
¼ cup of flax seeds, finely ground
¼ cup of vegan peanut butter
½ cup of vegan chocolate chips

Directions:
1. In your food processor, mix chickpeas with a pinch of salt, baking soda and powder, vanilla extract, flax seeds and vegan butter. Blend well.
2. Add chocolate chips, stir gently using a spatula, transfer the mix into a lined baking pan, then put it in the oven at 350 degrees F and bake for 30 minutes.
3. Take pan out of the oven, leave aside to cool down, cut, arrange on a platter, and serve.

Enjoy!

Nutritional value: 95 calories, 2 grams of fat, 15 grams of carbs, 1 gram of sugar, 3 grams of fiber, 2 grams of protein

# Special Strawberry and Rhubarb Pie
Surprise your loved ones with this!

Ingredients:
*For the crust:*
3 cups of blanched almond flour
2 teaspoons of vanilla extract
½ teaspoon of baking soda
½ cup of grapeseed oil
¼ cup of agave nectar
*For the filling:*
3 cups of rhubarb, roughly chopped
Zest from 1 orange, finely grated
1-pint strawberries, cut into halves
½ teaspoon of cinnamon
3 tablespoons of arrowroot powder
1/3 cup of agave nectar

Directions:
1. In a bowl, mix almond flour with a pinch of salt, baking soda, grapeseed oil, ¼ cup of agave nectar and 2 teaspoons of vanilla extract. Stir well.
2. Line a pie plate with parchment paper, grease it with some oil, pour half of the mix you've just made in a thin layer, then put the mix in the oven at 325 degrees F and bake for 15 minutes.
3. Meanwhile, shape a circle from the rest of the dough, place it on a round shaped parchment paper and then put it in the freezer and wait 15 minutes.
4. Take bottom pie crust out of the oven, leave aside to cool down and take the top crust out of the freezer and leave it aside.
5. Put rhubarb in a small pot, heat it up over medium heat, and cook for 10 minutes. Add 1/3 cup of agave nectar, cinnamon and orange zest. Stir and cook for 2 more minutes. Add strawberries, then stir and cook for 2 more minutes.
6. In a bowl, mix water with arrowroot, and stir well. Take rhubarb and strawberry mix off the heat, add arrowroot mix, and stir well. Pour this into the pie crust, top with the other pie crust, then put the pie in the oven at 325 degrees F for 10 minutes.

Nutritional value: 219 calories, 10 grams of fat, 54 grams of carbs, 3 grams of fiber, 32 grams of sugar, 2 grams of protein

# Vegan Apple Cheesecake

The autumn is all about strong flavors! What an adequate recipe for you to try this season!

Ingredients:
*For the crust:*
3 tablespoons of brown rice flour
4 tablespoons of sugar
3 cups of pecans
6 tablespoons of vegan margarine, melted
*For the filling:*
3 tubs of Tofutti
3 tablespoons of lemon juice
2 tablespoons of almond milk
19 ounces of extra firm tofu
1 teaspoon of vanilla bean paste
½ cup of brown sugar
¾ teaspoon of cloves
6 tablespoons of brown rice flour
1 ½ teaspoon of cinnamon
*For the topping:*
1 ½ cups of brown sugar
2 tablespoons of vegan margarine
3 apples, sliced
¼ cup of potato starch, mixed with ¼ cup of cold water

Directions:
1. In your food processor, mix pecans with 4 tablespoons of sugar, 3 tablespoons of brown rice flour and 6 tablespoons of already melted vegan margarine. Blend well.
2. Transfer this to a spring from pan, press well on the bottom, then put the mix in the oven at 400 degrees F, bake for 13 minutes, then take the food out of the oven and leave it aside to cool down.
3. In a bowl, mix almond milk with 3 tablespoons of lemon juice, 3 tubs of Tofutti, extra firm tofu, vanilla bean paste, ½ cup of brown sugar, 1 ½ teaspoon of cinnamon, ¾ teaspoon of cloves and 6 tablespoons of rice flour. Stir.
4. Transfer this mix to your food processor and blend it well.

5. Pour the mix into the baked crust, then put the cake in the oven at 325 degrees F and bake for 70 minutes.
6. Turn off heat, leave cheesecake inside for 1 more hour, take out of the oven, leave aside to cool down, put in the fridge and keep it there until you serve.
7. Put 2 tablespoons of cold margarine in a pan and melt it over medium-high heat, add apples, 1 ½ cups of brown sugar and potato starch mixed with water. Stir well, take off heat and leave aside to cool down.
8. Pour the mix over the cheesecake, spread evenly, then put the cake in the fridge for another few hours, and then serve.

Enjoy!

Nutritional value: 450 calories, 21 grams of fat, 66 grams of carbs, 2 grams of fiber, 38 grams of sugar, 7 grams of protein

# Vegan Black Bean Brownies
## They are simply delicious!

Ingredients:
1 ¾ cups of canned black beans, drained and rinsed
3 tablespoons of melted coconut oil
2 tablespoons of flaxseed meal, mixed with 6 tablespoons of water
¾ cup of cocoa powder
A pinch of salt
½ cup of organic cane sugar
1 teaspoon of vanilla extract
1 ½ teaspoon of baking powder

Directions:
1. Put flaxseed meal mixed with water into your food processor, and pulse well.
2. Add a pinch of salt, black beans, coconut oil, cocoa powder, baking powder and vanilla extract, and pulse again well.
3. Pour this into a greased 12-piece muffin tray, then put the food in the oven at 350 degrees F and bake for 25 minutes.
4. Take muffins out of the oven, leave them to cool down, transfer them to a platter, and serve.
Enjoy!

Nutritional value: 79 calories, 3 grams of fat, 9 grams of carbs, 2 grams of fiber, 0 grams of sugar, 4 grams of protein

# Autumn Vegan Coconut Macaroons
Easy to make - you'll love them!

Ingredients:
2 tablespoons of agave syrup
2 tablespoons of raw sugar
2 tablespoons of orange marmalade
2 tablespoons of coconut milk
A pinch of sea salt
A pinch of ginger powder
1 cup of dried coconut flakes
¾ teaspoon of baking powder
¼ cup of brown rice flour
¼ cup of cranberries
¼ cup of pistachios, chopped

Directions:
1. In a bowl, mix agave syrup with orange marmalade, raw sugar, coconut milk, sea salt, and ginger powder, and stir well.
2. In another bowl, mix coconut flakes with rice flour, baking powder, cranberries, and pistachios.
3. Combine the 2 mixtures, stir well, cover it and then let it chill in the fridge for 15 minutes.
4. Line a baking sheet with parchment paper.
5. Scoop, on a baking sheet, spoonfuls of batter, press macaroons. Then put the food in the oven at 350 degrees F and bake for 16 minutes.
6. Take macaroons out of the oven to cool down for 5-6 minutes, then transfer them to a platter, and serve.

Enjoy!

Nutritional value: 72 calories, 3 grams of fat, 10 grams of carbs, 1 gram of fiber, 5 grams of sugar, 1 gram of protein

## Vegan Blueberry and Rosemary Dessert
It's such a savory autumn dessert! Try it!

Ingredients:
2 cups of garbanzo bean flour
2 cups of rolled oats
8 cups of blueberries
1 stick of vegan butter
1 cup of walnuts
3 tablespoons of maple syrup
A pinch of salt
2 tablespoons of fresh rosemary, chopped

Directions:
1. Spread blueberries in a greased baking pan, and leave aside for now.
2. Meanwhile, in your food processor, mix rolled oats with bean flour, walnuts, vegan butter, maple syrup, a pinch of salt and rosemary. Blend well.
3. Layer this mix over blueberries, then put everything in the oven at 350 degrees F and bake for 30 minutes.
4. Take dessert out of the oven, leave aside to cool down, then cut and serve.

Enjoy!

Nutritional value: 250 calories, 6 grams of fat, 28 grams of carbs, 5 grams of sugar, 1 gram of fiber, 3 grams of protein

# Vegan Raspberry and Corn Muffins
These muffins are the best!

Ingredients:
3 tablespoons of corn starch
1 cup of millet- chia flour
1 cup of yellow corn meal
2 tablespoons of raw sugar
½ teaspoon of baking soda
A pinch of salt
2 teaspoons of baking powder
1 cup of soy milk
¼ cup of water
½ cup of applesauce
1 tablespoon of lemon juice
6 ounces of raspberries

Directions:
1. In a bowl, mix millet-chia flour with corn meal, corn starch, baking soda and powder and a pinch of salt. Stir well.
2. In another bowl, put soy milk with applesauce, water, lemon juice and raspberries. Stir well.
3. Combine the 2 mixtures, stir well, pour this into a 12 piece lined muffin tray, then put the food in the oven at 375 degrees F and bake for 25 minutes.
4. Take muffins out of the oven, leave them to cool down, arrange on a platter, and serve them. Enjoy!

Nutritional value: 109 calories, 1 gram of fat, 21 grams of carbs, 3 grams of sugar, 3 grams of fiber, 3 grams of protein

# Vegan Ganache Cake
An elegant vegan dessert perfect for a party!

Ingredients:
12 ounces of dried apricots
2 tablespoons of chia seeds
1 tablespoon of cocoa nibs
1 ½ tablespoon of coconut oil
A pinch of salt
2 tablespoons of almond butter
*For the filling:*
4 avocados, pitted
5 ounces of coconut oil, melted
5 ounces of raw cocoa
3 ounces of maple syrup
2 tablespoons of raw sugar
1 teaspoon of salt
1 tablespoon of vanilla essence

Directions:
1. In your food processor, mix apricots with chia seeds, cocoa nibs, a pinch of salt, and almond butter. Blend well.
2. Add 1 ½ tablespoon of coconut oil, blend again, transfer everything to a silicone dish, and press well.
3. Clean your food processor, then place in it the avocados, 5 ounces of coconut oil, 5 ounces of raw cocoa, 3 ounces of maple syrup, 2 tablespoons of raw sugar, salt, and vanilla essence. Blend well.
4. Pour this over cake base, spread evenly and keep the cake in the fridge for a few hours.
5. Cut and serve the cake.

Enjoy!

Nutritional value: 160 calories, 2 grams of fat, 22 grams of carbs, 1 gram of fiber, 13 grams of sugar, 1 gram of protein

# Vegan Saffron Pudding
This is a Persian style dessert that you need to try!

Ingredients:
*For the pudding:*
1 cup of water + ¼ cup of hot water
3 cups of coconut milk
½ cup of raw sugar
¾ cup of brown rice flour
2-star anise
1 cinnamon stick
12 cardamom pods
½ teaspoon of saffron
½ teaspoon of turmeric
*For the syrup:*
3 tablespoons of water
½ cup of raw sugar
2 tablespoons of orange blossom water
Gold raisins for serving
Pistachios for serving

Directions:
1. In a bowl, mix the cinnamon stick with cardamom, star anise, turmeric, and saffron.
2. Add ¼ cup of hot water, and leave aside.
3. Put 3 cups of coconut milk in a pan and heat it up over medium-high heat.
4. Add 1 cup of water, ½ cup of sugar, and stir.
5. Bring to a boil, add rice flour gradually, and stir until it thickens.
6. Add soaked spices, then cook and stir for 20 minutes.
7. Take pudding off heat, strain it into a bowl, and divide it into 6 small dishes.
8. Meanwhile, heat up a pan over medium heat, add 3 tablespoons of water, ½ cup of sugar, and orange blossom water, and bring to a boil.
9. Take off heat, then pour the liquid over the puddings.
10. Top each pudding with pistachios, raisins, and saffron threads. Serve right away.

Nutritional value: 222 calories, 1 gram of fat, 29 grams of carbs, 14 grams of sugar, 0 grams of fiber, 1 gram of protein

# Vegan Sweet Potato Pudding
Presentable and delicious!

Ingredients:
3 sweet potatoes
3 tablespoons of maple syrup
1 teaspoon of vanilla extract
A pinch of sea salt
½ cup of coconut milk

Directions:
1. Prick potatoes, arrange them on a baking sheet, then put them in the oven at 400 degrees F and bake for 45 minutes.
2. Take them out of the oven, leave them aside to cool down for 20 minutes, cut them, scoop the flesh out and put it into your food processor.
3. Add salt, maple syrup, coconut milk, and vanilla. Blend well.
4. Transfer the pudding into small dessert bowls, and serve right away.

Enjoy!

Nutritional value: 89 calories, 1 gram of fat, 19 grams of carbs, 2 grams of fiber, 8 grams of sugar, 1 gram of protein

# Autumn Vegan Chocolate Pudding
One of the best autumn dessert choices!

Ingredients:
1 cup of soy milk
2 tablespoons of cornstarch
1 cup of soy creamer
½ cup of sugar
3 tablespoons of egg replacer
2 teaspoons of vanilla extract
3 ounces of vegan chocolate, chopped
3 tablespoons of egg replacer

Directions:
1. Put soy milk, soy creamer and cornstarch in a pan, heat it up over medium heat, and stir.
2. Add sugar, stir well again, bring to a boil, and take off heat.
3. In a bowl, mix egg replacer with ¼ cup of boiled mix, stir well, and pour into the pan.
4. Return everything to heat for 4 minutes and stir until it thickens.
5. In a bowl, mix vegan chocolate with the hot mix, stir, and leave aside for 1 minute.
6. Stir again, leave aside for 15 minutes and then mix in vanilla.
7. Pour the mix into dessert cups and then put them in the fridge and wait 3 hours. Serve when ready.

Enjoy!

Nutritional value: 101 calories, 1 gram of fat, 15 grams of carbs, 3 grams of fiber, 12 grams of sugar, 8 grams of protein

# A True Vegan Pumpkin Pudding
There's nothing like a pumpkin pudding to help you celebrate autumn!

Ingredients:
1 2/3 cups of almond milk
1 can of pumpkin puree
2 tablespoons of maple syrup
3 tablespoons of cornstarch
½ teaspoon of cinnamon
¼ cup of brown sugar
½ teaspoon of nutmeg
Walnuts, chopped for serving
Soy whipped cream for serving

Directions:
1. In a bowl, mix almond milk with pumpkin puree, maple syrup, cornstarch, cinnamon, and nutmeg. Stir well.
2. Transfer this into a pan, heat it up over medium heat and cook for 8 minutes until it thickens.
3. Pour into dessert cups, keep in the fridge for 1 hour and 30 minutes and then serve with chopped walnuts and soy whipped cream on top.

Enjoy!

Nutritional value: 349 calories, 4 grams of fat, 70 grams of carbs, 23 grams of fiber, 28 grams of sugar, 10 grams of protein

# Autumn Vegan Bread Pudding
## One of the best puddings!

Ingredients:
5 cups of bread cubes
2 ¼ cups of soy milk
2 tablespoons of maple syrup
½ cup of brown sugar
¼ cup of raisins
1 teaspoon of vanilla
A pinch of cinnamon

Directions:
1. In a bowl, mix sugar with soy milk, vanilla, and maple syrup. Stir well.
2. Add bread cubes, stir gently, and leave aside for 10 minutes.
3. Add a pinch of cinnamon and raisins, and gently stir again.
4. Pour this into a greased baking dish, then put the dish in the oven at 350 degrees F and bake for 45 minutes.
5. Leave pudding to completely cool down before cutting and serving it.

Enjoy!

Nutritional value: 174 calories, 18 grams of fat, 34 grams of carbs, 1 gram of fiber, 20 grams of sugar, 4 grams of protein

# Vegan Pumpkin Smoothie
This will give you so much energy and a lot of nutritious elements!

Ingredients:
1 banana
1 cup of almond milk
¼ teaspoon of pumpkin pie spice
1 scoop of vanilla bean protein powder
¼ teaspoon of cinnamon
2 tablespoons of maple syrup
2/3 cup of pumpkin puree

Directions:
1. In your kitchen blender, mix banana with almond milk, vanilla bean protein powder, pumpkin pie spice, and cinnamon. Blend well.
2. Add maple syrup and pumpkin puree. Blend again well.
3. Transfer the mix into a tall glass and serve right away.

Enjoy!

Nutritional value: 158 calories, 5 grams of fat, 23 grams of carbs, 4 grams of fiber, 12 grams of sugar, 5 grams of protein

# Chapter 4. Vegan Desserts for Winter

## Vegan Ice Cream Sandwich
Why shouldn't you enjoy such a dessert in the winter?

Ingredients:
*For the cookies:*
½ teaspoon of cinnamon
2 teaspoons of Chinese five spice
1 cup of almonds
A pinch of salt
8 dates, pitted
2 ½ tablespoons of cocoa powder
6 tablespoons of coconut oil, melted
*For the ice cream:*
¾ can of coconut cream
2 frozen bananas
4 tablespoons of tahini
1 tablespoon of grated ginger
1/3 cup of maple syrup
A pinch of salt
1/3 cup of coconut oil, melted

Directions:
1. In your food processor, mix almonds with five spice, cinnamon, dates, a pinch of salt, cocoa powder, and coconut oil. Blend well.
2. Shape two balls with your hands, wrap them in foil, then put them in the freezer and wait 10 minutes.
3. Take balls out of the freezers, roll them out, cut 4 pieces with a cookie cutter and place them on a plate.
4. Repeat this with the rest of the dough but leave these pieces in the cookie cutters.
5. Arrange all pieces, including the ones in the cookie cutters on a lined tray and keep them in the freezer for 10 minutes.
6. Meanwhile, in your food processor, mix bananas with the coconut cream, ginger, tahini, 1/3 cup of maple syrup, a pinch of salt and 1/3 cup of coconut oil. Blend well.

7. Take cookies out of the freezer, spread ice cream on the first 4 pieces, top them with the other 4 pieces from the bottom of the cookie cutters, then put them in the freezer and wait 4 hours before you serve them.
8. Remove the cookie cutters 10 minutes before you serve them.

Enjoy!

Nutritional value: 240 calories, 14 grams of fat, 44 grams of carbs, 3 grams of fiber, 14 grams of sugar, 4 grams of protein

# Delicious Vegan Pomegranate Fudge
## Irresistible!

Ingredients:
½ cup of condensed coconut milk
1 teaspoon of vanilla extract
1 ½ cups of vegan chocolate, roughly chopped
½ cup of almonds, chopped
½ cup of pomegranate arils
A pinch of salt

Directions:
1. Put milk in a pan and heat it up over medium-low heat.
2. Add chocolate, and stir for 5 minutes.
3. Take off heat. Add vanilla extract, half of the pomegranate arils and half the of the nuts. Stir.
4. Pour this into a lined baking pan, spread, sprinkle a pinch of salt and the rest of the pomegranate arils and nuts, cover, and put the food in the fridge and wait a few hours.
5. Cut, arrange on a platter and serve.

Enjoy!

Nutritional value: 68 calories, 0 grams of fat, 15 grams of carbs, 14 grams of sugar, 0 grams of protein

# Vegan Caramel Apples
## An amazing winter dessert!

Ingredients:
16 dates, soaked for 10 minutes
1 tablespoon of peanut butter
¼ cup of almond milk
1 teaspoon of vanilla extract
4 big apples
Melted vegan chocolate for serving
Chopped pecans for serving

Directions:
1. Put dates in your food processor, and pulse a few times.
2. Add milk, vanilla extract and peanut butter. Blend well.
3. Push a stick in the center of each apple, spread caramel mix that you've made all over them and roll them into the melted vegan chocolate and chopped pecans.
4. Arrange them on a platter, and serve.

Enjoy!

Nutritional value: 200 calories, 0 grams of fat, 43 grams of carbs, 6 grams of fiber, 12 grams of sugar, 1 gram of protein

# Vegan Winter Cheesecake
It's satisfying winter dessert!

Ingredients:
*For the white layer:*
6 tablespoons of lemon juice
1 ½ cups of cashews, soaked overnight
6 tablespoons of maple syrup
1 teaspoon of vanilla extract
5 tablespoons of coconut oil
*For the yellow layer:*
½ teaspoon of cinnamon
1 ½ teaspoon of turmeric
1 cup of mango, chopped
*For the orange layer:*
1 ½ carrots, chopped
1 cup of dried apricots
1 tablespoon of lemon juice
2 tablespoons of coconut oil, melted
1 tablespoon of maple syrup
1 teaspoon of cinnamon

Directions:
1. In your blender, mix 1½ cups of cashews with 6 tablespoons of lemon juice, 6 tablespoons of maple syrup, 5 tablespoons of coconut oil, a pinch of salt and 1 teaspoon of vanilla extract. Blend well, then transfer the mix into a bowl and leave it aside.
2. Clean your food processor, then add 1 cup of mango to it. Mix with turmeric and cinnamon. Blend well, then transfer the mix into a bowl and leave it aside. Clean your food processor again and add apricots. Mix with carrots, 2 tablespoons of coconut oil, 1 tablespoon of lemon juice, 1 tablespoon of maple syrup, 1 teaspoon of cinnamon and a pinch of turmeric. Blend well and transfer the mix into a third bowl. Spread the orange layer evenly on the bottom of a springform pan. Pour the yellow layer on top, and spread well. End with the white layer, spread, keep cheesecake in the freezer for 6 hours, cut and serve it.

Nutritional value: 170 calories, 12 grams of fat, 32 grams of carbs, 5 grams of fiber, 1 gram of sugar, 12 grams of protein

# Winter Pumpkin Custard
## For a cold winter day!

Ingredients:
1 ½ cups of pumpkin puree
2/3 cup of coconut sugar
1 cup of coconut milk
2 tablespoons of chia seeds ground and mixed with 5 tablespoons of water
1 tablespoon of baking powder
2 teaspoons of pumpkin pie spice
A pinch of salt
1 teaspoon of cinnamon
½ teaspoon of vanilla
Pumpkin seeds for serving

Directions:
1. In a bowl, mix pumpkin puree with coconut milk, coconut sugar, chia seeds mixed with water, baking powder, pumpkin pie spice, a pinch of salt, cinnamon and vanilla. Stir well using your kitchen mixer.
2. Pour this into small ramekins, arrange them on a baking tray filled half way with hot water, then put the food in the oven at 325 degrees F and bake for 1 hour.
3. Take custard out of the oven, leave it to cool down, and serve with pumpkin seeds on top. Enjoy!

Nutritional value: 151 calories, 2 grams of fat, 26 grams of carbs, 2 grams of fiber, 12 grams of sugar, 6 grams of protein

# Vegan Chestnut and Cashew Trifles
Truly addictive!

Ingredients:
*For the cream:*
3 tablespoons of agave nectar
3 tablespoons of water
A pinch of salt
Juice from ½ orange
½ teaspoon of orange extract
5 ounces of cashews, soaked in hot water for 4 hours
*For the filling:*
8 dates, pitted
3 ounces of water
8 ounces of already cooked chestnuts
1 ½ teaspoon of vanilla extract
A pinch of pink salt
*For the base:*
2.5 ounces of pistachio kernels
2 ounces of cocoa nibs
2 ounces of coconut
1 tablespoon of cocoa powder
4 dates, pitted
Zest from 1 orange
2 figs, cut into wedges for serving

Directions:
1. Drain cashews and put them in your kitchen blender.
2. Add salt, water, orange juice, orange extract and agave nectar. Blend well, then put the food in the fridge.
3. Meanwhile, put the already cooked chestnuts in your food processor.
4. Add a pinch of salt, vanilla extract, 8 dates and 3 ounces of water. Blend well and then put the mix in the fridge until you use it.
5. In your food processor, mix pistachio kernels with coconut, cocoa powder, and cocoa nibs. Pulse well.
6. Add 4 dates and zest from 1 orange, and pulse well again.

7. Divide this last mix between 6 trifle dishes, and press well.
8. Add chestnut mix, and top with cashew cream.
9. Serve with figs wedges.

Enjoy!

Nutritional value: 439 calories, 21 grams of fat, 51 grams of carbs, 36 grams of sugar, 8 grams of fiber, 9 grams of protein

# Winter Berry and Cashew Cake
Smooth and delicious!

Ingredients:
*For the crust:*
½ cup of dates, pitted
1 tablespoon of water
½ teaspoon of vanilla
½ cup of almonds
*For the cake:*
2 ½ cups of cashews, soaked for 8 hours
1 cup of blueberries
¾ cup of maple syrup
1 tablespoon of coconut oil

Directions:
1. In your food processor, mix dates with water, vanilla, and almonds. Pulse well.
2. Transfer dough to a working surface, then flatten it.
3. Arrange into a lined round pan and leave aside.
4. In your blender, mix maple syrup with coconut oil, cashews, and blueberries. Blend well.
5. Spread the mix evenly on the crust, then put the cake in the freezer for 5 hours, leave at room temperature for 15 minutes, then cut and serve it.

Enjoy!

Nutritional value: 230 calories, 0 grams of fat, 12 grams of carbs, 4 grams of fiber, 43 grams of sugar, 4 grams of protein

# Winter Vegan Fruit Jelly
Everyone loves this vegan fruit jelly!

Ingredients:
1 pound of grapefruit jelly
½ pound of coconut yogurt.
A handful of fresh berries for serving
A handful of nuts, roughly chopped for serving

Directions:
1. In your food processor, combine grapefruit jelly with coconut yogurt. Blend well.
2. Add berries and nuts, toss gently, then transfer the mix into dessert cups, and serve right away!

Enjoy!

Nutritional value: 70 calories, 29 grams of fat, 4 grams of carbs, 1 gram of fiber, 3 grams of protein, 1 gram of sugar

# Vegan Winter Couscous Delight
In the mood for something unique? Then this is the dessert you have to try!

Ingredients:
¾ cup of couscous
¾ cup of water
A pinch of salt
13 ounces of canned coconut milk
1 teaspoon of vanilla
1 cardamom pod crushed
4 tablespoons of raw sugar
½ teaspoon of cinnamon
4 tablespoons of raisins

Directions:
1. Put water in a pot and heat it up over medium heat.
2. Add a pinch of salt, stir, take off heat, and add couscous.
3. Stir, cover, and leave aside for 5 minutes.
4. Fluff, and leave aside for now.
5. Put coconut milk in another pot and heat it up over medium heat.
6. Add cardamom, vanilla and cinnamon. Stir and simmer for 10 minutes.
7. Add raisins and couscous. Stir, then take off heat.
8. Leave aside to cool down for 10 minutes, transfer to dessert cups, and serve.

Enjoy!

Nutritional value: 176 calories, 10 grams of fat, 34 grams of carbs, 3 grams of fiber, 6 grams of protein, 2 grams of sugar

# Vegan Almond and Fig Winter Dessert
One of the easiest winter vegan desserts to make!

Ingredients:
2 tablespoons of coconut butter
12 figs, cut into halves
¼ cup of palm sugar
1 cup of almonds, toasted and chopped

Directions:
1. Heat up a pot with the butter over medium-high heat and stir until it melts.
2. Add sugar and figs. Stir well and cook for about 5 minutes.
3. Add almonds, stir gently, and take off heat.
4. Transfer the mix into dessert bowls, and serve right away!

Enjoy!

Nutritional value: 220 calories, 16 grams of fat, 39 grams of carbs, 6 grams of fiber, 9 grams of protein, 5 grams of sugar

# Vegan Winter Sponge Cake
It suits perfectly a winter meal!

Ingredients:
3 teaspoons of baking powder
1 teaspoon of baking soda
3 cups of almond flour
1 ½ cups of soy milk
½ cup of cornstarch
1 cup of vegetable oil
1 2/3 cup of palm sugar
2 cups of water
2 teaspoons of vanilla extract
¼ cup of lemon juice
Cooking spray for the pan

Directions:
1. In a bowl, mix almond flour with baking powder and soda, cornstarch and sugar. Stir well.
2. In a second bowl, mix oil with milk, vanilla extract, water and lemon juice. Stir.
3. Combine the 2 mixtures, stir, pour in a greased baking dish, then put the food in the oven at 357 degrees F and bake for 20 minutes.
4. Take out of the oven, leave aside to completely cool down, cut and serve right away.

Enjoy!

Nutritional value: 346 calories, 16 grams of fat, 47 grams of carbs, 0 grams of fiber, 2 grams of protein

# Vegan Fruit Mix
This amazing vegan dessert will warm up your winter days!

Ingredients:
1 cup of orange juice
A pinch of salt
1 pound of strawberries, cut into halves
1 ½ tablespoons of palm sugar
1 peach, cut into medium wedges
1 kiwi, cut into medium wedges
1 ½ tablespoons of champagne vinegar
1 tablespoon of extra virgin olive oil
1 ½ cups of blueberries
¼ cup of basil leaves, roughly chopped

Directions:
1. Put orange juice and vinegar in a pot and heat it up over medium-high heat.
2. Bring to a boil, simmer for 15 minutes, add oil, salt, stir, take off heat, and leave aside for 4 minutes.
3. Meanwhile, in a bowl, mix blueberries with strawberries, kiwi, and peach wedges.
4. Add orange vinaigrette, toss to coat, add basil on top, and serve right away!

Enjoy!

Nutritional value: 143 calories, 4 grams of fat, 32 grams of carbs, 4 grams of fiber, 2 grams of protein, 12 grams of sugar

## Special Winter Cherry Sorbet
It has a unique and tasty flavor!

Ingredients:
½ cup of vegan cocoa
A pinch of salt
2 cups of water
¾ cup of red cherry jam
¼ cup of palm sugar
*For the compote:*
¼ cup of palm sugar
1 pound of cherries, pitted and cut into halves

Directions:
1. Put cherry jam in a pot and mix with cocoa, ¼ cup of sugar and a pinch of salt.
2. Stir well, and bring to a boil over medium heat.
3. Add water, stir again, take off heat and leave aside to cool down completely.
4. Pour in a casserole and then put it in the freezer and wait 1 hour.
5. Meanwhile, in a bowl, mix ¼ cup of palm sugar with cherries. Stir, then leave aside for 1 hour.
6. When the time has passed, serve this compote with the sorbet.

Enjoy!

Nutritional value: 177 calories, 1 gram of fat, 30 grams of carbs, 3 grams of fiber, 1 gram of protein, 1 gram of sugar

# Winter Persimmon Bars
Simply delightful!

Ingredients:
*For the bars:*
1 cup of whole wheat flour
1 cup of white flour
A pinch of salt
2 teaspoons of cinnamon
1 teaspoon of baking soda
¾ cup of coconut sugar
2 tablespoons of flax seeds, mixed with 5 tablespoons of water
1/3 cup of canola oil
1 cup of persimmon pulp, mashed
½ cup of almond milk
¼ cup of coconut yogurt
1 cup of dates, pitted and chopped
1 teaspoon of vanilla extract
Cooking spray for the pan
*For the brown frosting:*
4 ounces of vegan butter
1 ½ cups of raw organic sugar
3 tablespoons of almond milk
1 teaspoon of orange zest
1 tablespoon of orange juice
1 teaspoon of vanilla extract

Directions:
1. In a bowl, mix flours with salt and baking soda. Stir, and leave aside.
2. In another bowl, mix flax seeds and water with oil, ¾ cup of coconut sugar. Stir well.
3. Add persimmon, ½ cup of almond milk, vegan yogurt and 1 teaspoon of vanilla extract. Stir well.
4. Combine flour mix with persimmon mix. Stir, and add dates at the end.
5. Stir again, pour this evenly into a pan greased with some cooking spray, then put it in the oven at 350 degrees F and bake for 25 minutes.
6. Meanwhile, put vegan butter in a pan and melt it over medium heat.
7. Stir, leave on stove for 10 minutes and then transfer it into a bowl.

8. Add 1 ½ cups of raw sugar, add orange zest, orange juice, 3 tablespoons of almond milk and 1 teaspoon of vanilla extract. Stir well.
9. Take pan out of the oven, leave aside to cool down for a few minutes, spread frosting all over, cut into 16 pieces, arrange on a platter, and serve.

Enjoy!

Nutritional value: 152 calories, 6 grams of fat, 24 grams of carbs, 1 gram of fiber, 12 grams of sugar, 2 grams of protein

# Winter Vegan Crème Brule
It tastes so much better than the non-vegan one!

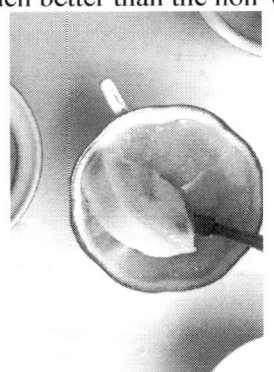

Ingredients:
1/3 cup of water
5 ounces of coconut milk
5 tablespoons of raw sugar
1 ½ tablespoon of cornstarch
1 ½ tablespoon of egg replacer powder
½ vanilla bean caviar
½ teaspoon of nutritional yeast
A pinch of salt
Sugar for the caramel

Directions:
1. In your food processor, mix water with coconut milk, egg replacer, vanilla bean caviar, yeast, cornstarch and a pinch of salt. Blend well.
2. Pour this into a pan and then place the pan on the stove on low heat.
3. Mix until it thickens, then pour into 4 ramekins.
4. Place ramekins in a dish, fill it half way with water, then put everything in the oven at 325 degrees F and bake for 35 minutes.
5. Take ramekins out of the oven, leave them aside for 2 hours, then sprinkle sugar all over them and melt it with a small kitchen torch.
6. Serve right away.
   Enjoy!

Nutritional value: 87 calories, 1 gram of fat, 10 grams of carbs, 0 grams of fiber, 7 grams of sugar, 4 grams of protein

# Vegan Tomato and Chocolate Cupcakes
One of the tastiest combinations!

Ingredients:
*for the cakes:*
½ cup of coconut sugar
¾ cup of white flour
½ teaspoon of baking soda
¼ cup of cocoa powder
½ teaspoon of baking powder
A pinch of salt
¼ cup of tomatoes, pureed
1 teaspoon of vanilla extract
2 tablespoons of raw pecan butter
1 tablespoons of apple cider vinegar
¼ cup of filtered water
*For the frosting:*
1/3 cup of cocoa powder
¾ cup of pecan butter
¼ cup of maple syrup
¼ cup of filtered water
A pinch of salt

Directions:
1. In a bowl, mix white flour with cocoa powder, baking soda, baking powder and a pinch of salt. Stir.
2. In another bowl, mix ½ cup of sugar with pureed tomatoes, 2 tablespoons of pecan butter, 1 teaspoon of vanilla extract ¼ cup of filtered water. Stir well.
3. Combine the 2 mixtures. Stir, and add the vinegar.
4. Stir well, pour this into a lined muffin tray, then put the food in the oven at 375 degrees F and bake for 15 minutes.
5. Take cupcakes out of the oven, leave them to cool down, and arrange them on a platter.
6. In a bowl, mix ¾ cup of pecan butter with 1/3 cup of cocoa powder, ¼ cup of filtered water, a pinch of salt ¼ cup of maple syrup. Stir well.
7. Pour this over cold cupcake, and serve.

Enjoy!

Nutritional value: 167 calories, 10 grams of fat, 25 grams of carbs, 1 gram of fiber, 0 grams of sugar, 2 grams of protein

# Winter Vegan Tomato Cake
## Something really different and new!

Ingredients:
1 ½ cups of whole wheat flour
1 teaspoon of cinnamon
1 teaspoon of baking powder
1 teaspoon of baking soda
A pinch of salt
¾ cup of brown sugar
1 cup of tomatoes, chopped
½ cup of extra virgin olive oil
2 tablespoons apple cider vinegar

Directions:
1. In a bowl, mix whole wheat flour with baking powder, baking soda, a pinch of salt, cinnamon and brown sugar. Stir well.
2. In another bowl, mix tomatoes with olive oil and vinegar. Stir well.
3. Combine the 2 mixtures. Stir well, and pour everything into a greased round pan.
4. Put the cake in the oven at 375 degrees F and bake for 30 minutes.
5. Take cake out of the oven, leave aside to cool down, transfer to a platter, cut and serve it.

Enjoy!

Nutritional value: 153 calories, 3 grams of fat, 28 grams of carbs, 0 grams of fiber, 11 grams of sugar, 2 grams of protein

# Winter Nectarines and Olive Oil Cake
What are you waiting for? Go and purchase the ingredients!

Ingredients:
2 cups of white flour
1 teaspoon of baking powder
1 teaspoon of baking soda
A pinch of salt
¾ cup of maple syrup
½ cup of extra virgin olive oil
¾ cup of water
2 tablespoons of lemon zest
¼ cup of lemon juice
2 nectarines, thinly sliced
1 tablespoon of lemon extract

Directions:
1. In a bowl, mix flour with baking powder, baking soda and salt. Stir well.
2. In a second bowl, mix oil with water, maple syrup, lemon zest, juice, and extract. Stir well.
3. Combine the 2 mixtures, and stir gently.
4. Pour batter into a Bundt pan, then put it in the oven at 350 degrees F and bake for 30 minutes.
5. Take cake out of the oven, and leave aside to cool down.
6. Meanwhile, heat up your kitchen grill over medium-high heat, brush nectarines with some olive oil, arrange them on a grill and cook for 3 minutes.
7. Cut cake, arrange on dessert plates and top with grilled nectarines.

Enjoy!

Nutritional value: 250 calories, 3 grams of fat, 52 grams of carbs, 1 gram of fiber, 12 grams of sugar, 5 grams of protein

# Vegan Butternut Cake
A modern vegan cake!

Ingredients:
*For the cake:*
1 teaspoon of cinnamon
1 teaspoon of apple cider vinegar
¾ cup of almond milk
2 ¼ cup of spelt flour
A pinch of salt
1 teaspoon of mixed spices
2 teaspoons of baking powder
½ teaspoon of baking soda
½ cup of butternut puree
1 teaspoon of vanilla extract
Zest from 1 orange
¾ cup of maple syrup
¼ cup of olive oil
*For the filling:*
1 cup of almonds, finely ground
1 teaspoon of vanilla extract
1/3 cup of almond milk
1 tablespoon of coconut milk
2 tablespoons of maple syrup
Juice from ½ lemon
Fruit marmalade

Directions:
1. Grease 2 baking tins, and leave aside.
2. In a bowl, mix almond milk with vinegar. Stir, then leave aside.
3. In another bowl, mix flour with spices, baking soda and powder, and salt. Stir.
4. In a third bowl, mix almond milk and vinegar with butternut puree, vanilla, maple syrup, orange zest and olive oil. Stir well.
5. Combine flour and milk mixtures. Stir well.
6. Pour this into greased pans, then put the food in the oven at 350 degrees F and bake for 25 minutes.

7. Take cakes out of the oven, leave them aside to cool down, then put them in the freezer and keep them there for 15 minutes.
8. Meanwhile, in a bowl, mix almonds with 1/3 cup of almond milk, 1 tablespoon of coconut oil, 1 teaspoon of vanilla extract, lemon juice, marmalade and 2 tablespoons of maple syrup. Stir well.
9. Take cakes out of the freezer, spread filling on one piece, top with the second one, cut and serve it.

Enjoy!

Nutritional value: 204 calories, 1 gram of fat, 40 grams of carbs, 14 grams of fiber, 2 grams of sugar, 10 grams of protein

# Winter Vegan Rum Cake
It's a winter dessert which you can serve for Christmas!

Ingredients:
1 cup of pecans, chopped
1 package of vegan cake mix
4 units of egg replacer
½ cup of vegetable oil
½ cup of water
½ cup of light rum
½ cup of vegan buttery spread

Directions:
1. In a bowl, mix pecans with vegan cake mix, egg replacer, water, vegetable oil, rum and vegan buttery spread. Stir well.
2. Pour this into a Bundt pan, then put it in the oven at 325 degrees F and bake for 1 hour.
3. Transfer the food to a platter, leave aside to cool down, cut and serve it.

Enjoy!

Nutritional value: 155 calories, 8 grams of fat, 44 grams of carbs, 1 gram of fiber, 15 grams of sugar, 3 grams of protein

# Winter Vanilla Cake
You've got to love this fluffy vegan cake!

Ingredients:
1 cup of raw sugar
1 ¾ cups of white flour
A pinch of salt
1 teaspoon of baking soda
1 cup of soy milk
2 teaspoons of vanilla extract
1 tablespoon of white vinegar
1/3 cup of olive oil
*For the vanilla frosting:*
2 teaspoons of vanilla extract
4 tablespoons of almond milk
3 ¾ cups of powdered sugar
3 tablespoons of vegan butter
Strawberries, cut in half for garnishing

Directions:
1. In a bowl, mix flour with sugar, baking soda and a pinch of salt. Stir.
2. Add olive oil, 2 teaspoons of vanilla extract, vinegar and 1 cup of soy milk. Stir well.
3. Grease 2 cake tins with some coconut oil and pour the batter into them.
4. Put the food in the oven at 350 degrees F and bake for 30 minutes.
5. Take cakes out of the oven, and leave aside to cool down.
6. In a bowl, mix 3 ¾ cups of sugar with 3 tablespoons of vegan butter, 4 tablespoons of soy milk and 2 teaspoons of vanilla extract. Stir using your hand mixer.
7. Spread some of this mix on one cake piece, top with the second one, and cover the cake with the rest of the frosting.
8. Decorate with strawberry halves, and serve!

Enjoy!

Nutritional value: 180 calories, 7 grams of fat, 29 grams of carbs, 1 gram of fiber, 12 grams of sugar, 2 grams of protein

# Winter Marmalade Cake
## Simple but more than delicious!

Ingredients:
7 ounces of vegan butter + some for greasing the pan
4 tablespoons of raw organic sugar
2 oranges, thinly sliced + zest and juice from 2 oranges
7 ounces of coconut sugar
6 tablespoons of fruit marmalade
1 tablespoon of egg replacer
7 ounces of white flour
2 ounces of almond, finely chopped

Directions:
1. Grease a cake pan with some vegan butter, sprinkle 4 tablespoons of raw sugar on the bottom, spread evenly, and arrange orange slices.
2. In a bowl, mix vegan butter with coconut sugar, 3 tablespoons of marmalade and egg replacer. Stir.
3. Add flour, almonds, a pinch of salt, zest, and juice of 2 oranges. Stir well.
4. Pour this over the orange slices, then put the food in the oven at 350 degrees F and bake for 50 minutes.
5. Take cake out of the oven, leave aside to cool down, turn it on a platter, and leave aside again.
6. Put the rest of the marmalade in a pan and heat it up over medium heat.
7. Pour this over cake, spread, cut and serve right away.

Enjoy!

Nutritional value: 470 calories, 24 grams of fat, 6 grams of carbs, 54 grams of sugar, 6 grams of protein

# Winter Green Apple Pie Smoothie
This green smoothie is perfect for the cold season!

Ingredients:
1 big green apple, cut into medium cubes
12 ounces of silk tofu
1 cup of baby spinach
1 tablespoon of pure maple syrup
A pinch of cardamom
½ teaspoon of cinnamon
½ teaspoon of vanilla extract

Directions:
1. Put apple cubes in your food processor.
2. Add spinach, tofu, maple syrup, vanilla extract, cardamom, and cinnamon, and blend until you obtain a smooth cream.
3. Pour into 2 glasses, and serve right away!

Enjoy!

Nutritional value: 145 calories, 0 grams of fat, 33 grams of carbs, 3 grams of fiber, 9 grams of sugar, 2 grams of protein

# Winter Coconut and Clementine Smoothie
Fresh and tasty!

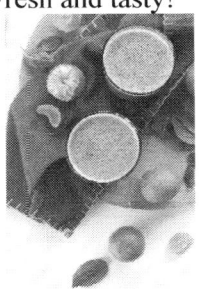

Ingredients:
1 banana, peeled and sliced
5 clementines, peeled and sliced
½ cup of coconut milk
1 handful of baby spinach
4 ice cubes
4 fresh mint leaves

Directions:
1. Put banana in your food processor.
2. Add clementines, coconut milk, baby spinach and ice cubes. Blend well.
3. Add mint leaves, blend some more, then transfer the mix into glasses, and serve.
Enjoy!

Nutritional value: 182 calories, 3 grams of fat, 40 grams of carbs, 29 grams of sugar, 3 grams of fiber, 3 grams of protein

Printed in Poland
by Amazon Fulfillment
Poland Sp. z o.o., Wrocław